C000163651

NAKED CAKES

NAKED CAKES

SIMPLY BEAUTIFUL
HANDMADE CREATIONS

Lyndel Miller

Photography by Mindi Cooke

weldon**owen**

Thank you to Handsome, Tahlia, and Sam. You are what makes everything beautiful in my world. I love you.

contents

contents

08

beauty in simplicity

I'M AN ENTERTAINER. I was brought up in a quintessential 1970s home on the northern beaches of Sydney, Australia, listening to Fleetwood Mac and hiding under tables while Boney M played on the stereo, and conga lines flowed through our laughter-filled home on my parents' party nights. When a party was announced, I would delight in my mother's enthusiasm and attention to every detail. The food was always at the heart, and the styling for the evening was complementary. If it was a modest barbecue, the vibe would be relaxed, carefree, and organic – no place settings, just plates and cutlery in piles, simple table linens, and a beautiful, flowing, rustic feel. Food was placed in the center of the table for all to share. Salads were served in stylish yet understated bowls. However, if it was a formal affair, then all the treasured family china came out, the glassware, crystal, and cutlery were polished, new taper candles were purchased, and fresh flowers were bought or picked from our garden (or dare I say, someone else's!). Considering her skill, it was no surprise that my mum ended up owning a café that, I am proud to say, became an institution in our home town.

My mother had Champagne taste and a beer kick. She loved the good things in life, but often couldn't afford them (with six kids and four jobs) so she made us feel like we had it all – and we felt like we did. She knew how to set a scene and make everyone feel welcome and warm. You could say food was her language of love. With a brood to feed, sometimes a birthday party was just a modest invitation for all our family and friends to visit and eat cake – not a full meal, but just an afternoon around the family table, indulging in a decadent cake and delighting in its beauty.

This is where my interest in food began, as well as my affection for nature and its gifts of fresh produce, not to mention my enjoyment of styling a scene, taking pride in being a hospitable host, and making the ordinary extraordinary. I am my mother's daughter!

I started out as a food stylist at health retreats, where the goal was to make the food both taste and look beautiful. Stuffed vegetables were a challenge to make appetizing, so I brought in edible flowers to use as props, as my mum used to do in her café. However, I soon realized that decorating cakes brought me the greatest joy in the kitchen – the scope for unleashing my creativity was almost limitless.

It wasn't until my wedding day some years later that I first saw a "naked" cake. My sister Sarah made a magnificent cake to fit the boho chic theme of my wedding (I'm a little bohemian at heart!). It was a tiered white-chocolate mud cake, soaked in liqueur, topped with buttercream, and crowned with fresh and exotic blooms and seashells. It was perfect – the most memorable gift I have ever received, and I was captivated by its sheer organic beauty. This is where my love affair with naked cakes began.

010

WHAT ARE NAKED CAKES? Naked cakes have been popping up everywhere in the last few years, and they are simply cakes that aren't covered in icing or frosting. Fondant-haters, lazy bakers, and time-poor hosts rejoice! Naked cakes are budget-friendly, DIY, and absolutely swoon-worthy. However, don't get me wrong – they are not frosting-free. They just use frosting in a different way and are filled with luscious buttercreams and topped with delectable treats for the taste buds. Some bakers and cake decorators may call this style of cake "unfinished," but I love the simple elegance of this undressed cake, especially when paired with the natural romance of flowers, foliage, delectable fruits, and other decorations.

Naked cakes come in all different shapes and sizes. They are beautiful, simple, and unpretentious. There is an unlimited number of elements that can be created and added to your cake, so the naked cake can transcend a number of different themes and styles for any event. These naturally textural cakes are popular for the bride wanting a rustic-themed wedding, or anyone who wants to add some sensual and organic flair to their home entertaining.

You can go for a naked cake that's clean and tidy and exercise your piping skills between cake layers, try a "whitewashed" look with a thin layer of buttercream swept over the surface, or go for a more eclectic and organic look. There is no wrong way. Whether you're a fan of a more towering creation or delight in a petite gateau, are hosting a sophisticated or a simple affair, these beauties don't play favorites.

Regardless of what you are celebrating, you can pick and choose your profile flavors, selecting from or adapting the abundance of suggestions within these pages, and make a showstopping, delicious, and beautiful creation that you can truly claim as your very own.

So many people are intimidated by the thought of putting together a tiered naked cake. There is no need to be. It is nothing like building a traditional tiered cake. Remember, there's no icing! Leave the traditional decorated cakes, with their fondant and frosting techniques, to the master bakers. The naked cake forgoes all of that traditionalism by choice. What's more, a naked cake need not be perfect. There is charm in its imperfections. The beauty of homemade reigns supreme. The naked cake is about beauty in simplicity.

There are three elements to the naked cakes in this book: the base, the fillings, and the toppings. However, I wanted to start the book with a selection of finished cakes (my "queens"), designed to excite and inspire you, and show you the possibilities.

THE QUEENS This chapter includes a selection of the most beautiful cakes I have made to date. They are my stars, all of them unique – from wholesome and feminine, to sexy, sophisticated, and even flamboyant. I chose cakes that would speak to each and every one of you, as beauty is in the eye of the beholder. There isn't a lady among them who wouldn't shine as the center of attention at your next event.

BASES TO INSPIRE When deciding on your own naked cake, the first element is the choice of base cake – consider it your canvas. In this chapter you will discover fourteen simple and versatile cakes. Most often, naked cakes tend to be made using a plain sponge or Madeira-style cake, but they don't

have to be – sometimes I like to make things a little more exciting. Explore this chapter, together with my simple flavor-pairing bible, "This goes with that" (page 12), and start to develop your cake and flavor profile. You can stick to a single flavor or mix to your heart's content. Create a single, double, or multi-tiered cake – I have also included tips and techniques to help you layer your cakes successfully.

FILLINGS & FROSTINGS The second step is to select the filling. In this section you will delight in exploring more than thirty-five delicious recipes for sensational buttercreams, glazes, creams, syrups, and more, for generously lining (or topping) the layers of your chosen cake. There is a flavor to suit every palate. If you are not sure where to begin, start with mascarpone buttercream (page 112). I guarantee you will be licking this off the spoon!

FINISHING TOUCHES The final element is the decorative topping, which I sometimes like to call the "crown." This might be a sweet creation, like praline or poached or candied fruit, or a crown of edible flowers or leaves. Of course, some of the flowers and foliage I have used are for decorative purposes only. Nonedible plants must never make contact with your cake. You need to do your research if you plan to use any plants as decoration. See page 161 for important safety information.

SETTING THE SCENE When party planning, some people begin with the dressing of the table and the decorations, and then they move on to the food. However, I generally start with the menu (as do the rest of my foodie family). But, having said that, I feel the scene you set is important and adds another layer to your dining experience. In the last chapters you will find how-tos for making your own colorful and elegant decorations, which will enhance any dining table or event room. I have also included four themed design stories, to inspire you to set the scene for a whole event, from the cake, food, and drinks to the table settings and room decorations.

BE INSPIRED Naked cakes speak volumes to me. While I appreciate the skills of a master chef, I don't aspire to be one. That style of cooking doesn't fit my lifestyle nor does it reflect it. I just love to create. The rustic nature of the naked cake offers an honesty and transports me back to my childhood. For me, naked cakes also bring a little joy back into handmade. Handmade is no longer considered dowdy or just a matter of making do. It's an opportunity to express your creativity and – if you are making something as a gift – your affection. My goal is to inspire and encourage. I could go all out and give directions for creating an elaborate affair, but I don't want people to feel intimidated. This book is all about keeping it simple, accessible, inviting, and fun.

I hope this book doesn't sit on shelves gathering dust. I want it to be passed around and enjoyed, the pages to become stained with ingredients and marked with personal notes and experience, offering you hours of fun, taking you to another level in the kitchen, helping you to discover the artist within.

011

Fondant-haters, lazy bakers, and time-poor hosts rejoice! Naked cakes are budget-friendly, DIY, and absolutely swoon-worthy.

012

This goes with that

BEFORE YOU SET OFF EXPLORING THE PAGES IN THIS BOOK, here is a little guide to help take the guesswork out of pairing your base cakes with the myriad fillings, frostings, and sweet finishes. It will not only inspire you to try the recipes in this book, but it will also send you on a culinary journey, sparking your imagination and getting your creative juices going. Try your hand at a few of these flavor combinations for delicious cakes that you and your family and friends will love. Enjoy experimenting, and I hope you discover some new flavor matches of your own to add to the list.

A

ALLSPICE GOES WITH:

Anise, Apple, Beet, Caramel, Cardamom, Chocolate, Cinnamon, Cloves, Coconut, Ginger, Nutmeg, Nuts, Pear, Pumpkin

ALMOND GOES WITH:

Apple, Apricot, Banana, Blood Orange, Caramel, Cardamom, Cherry, Chocolate, Cinnamon, Coffee, Currant, Date, Fig, Ginger, Honey, Orange, Peach, Pear, Plum, Rosewater

ANISE GOES WITH:

Allspice, Apple, Beet, Caramel, Carrot, Chocolate, Cinnamon, Citrus, Coconut, Cranberry, Dill, Fennel, Fig, Peach, Pomegranate, Pumpkin

APPLE GOES WITH:

Allspice, Almond, Anise, Beet, Caramel, Cardamom, Chestnut, Cinnamon, Cloves, Cranberry, Currant, Ginger, Hazelnut, Kiwi Fruit, Lime, Mandarin, Mango, Maple, Pear, Pomegranate, Rhubarb, Rosemary, Strawberry, Walnut

APRICOT GOES WITH:

Almond, Blackberry, Black Pepper, Caramel, Cardamom, Cherry, Elderberry, Ginger, Hazelnut, Honey, Lemon, Orange, Peach, Plum, Raspberry, Rhubarb, Vanilla, Walnut

B

BANANA GOES WITH:

Almond, Caramel, Cardamom, Cherry, Chocolate, Cinnamon, Coconut, Coffee, Ginger, Hazelnut, Honey, Kiwi Fruit, Mandarin, Mango, Papaya, Passion Fruit, Thyme, Walnut

BASIL GOES WITH:

Beet, Dill, Mint, Orange, Rosemary, Thyme

BEET GOES WITH:

Allspice, Anise, Apple, Basil, Black Pepper, Carrot, Cloves, Dill, Honey, Lemon, Mint, Orange, Pistachio Nut

BLACKBERRY GOES WITH:

Apricot, Black Pepper, Cinnamon, Elderberry, Gooseberry, Kiwi Fruit, Lemon, Mulberry, Peach, Plum, Raspberry, Rhubarb, Strawberry, Watermelon

BLACK PEPPER GOES WITH:

Apricot, Beet, Blackberry, Cardamom, Cherry, Coconut, Fig, Ginger, Grapefruit, Lemon, Plum, Rhubarb, Strawberry

BLOOD ORANGE GOES WITH:

Almond, Cardamom, Chocolate, Cinnamon, Citrus, Fig, Ginger, Honey

BLUEBERRY GOES WITH:

Cardamom, Elderberry, Fig, Ginger, Gooseberry, Kiwi Fruit, Lavender, Lemon, Mango, Mulberry, Raspberry, Rhubarb, Strawberry, Watermelon

BRAZIL NUT GOES WITH:

Caramel, Chocolate, Coconut, Ginger, Vanilla

014

C

CARAMEL GOES WITH:
Allspice, Almond, Anise, Apple, Apricot, Banana, Brazil Nut, Cardamom, Chestnut, Cinnamon, Coconut, Date, Ginger, Grapefruit, Hazelnut, Mandarin, Mango, Pear, Walnut

CARDAMOM GOES WITH:
Allspice, Apple, Apricot, Banana, Black Pepper, Blood Orange, Blueberry, Caramel, Chile, Cinnamon, Cloves, Coconut, Date, Fennel, Ginger, Lemon, Mandarin, Mango, Nuts, Pear, Rosewater

CARROT GOES WITH:
Anise, Beet, Cinnamon, Cloves, Dill, Ginger, Maple, Nutmeg, Orange, Raisin, Thyme, Walnut

CHERRY GOES WITH:
Almond, Apricot, Banana, Black Pepper, Chocolate, Cinnamon, Currant, Hazelnut, Kiwi Fruit, Lemon, Lime, Mandarin, Nectarine, Orange, Peach, Plum, Vanilla, White Chocolate

CHESTNUT GOES WITH:
Apple, Caramel, Chocolate, Coffee, Pear, Plum, Vanilla

CHILE GOES WITH:
Cardamom, Chocolate, Cinnamon, Mango, Watermelon

CHOCOLATE GOES WITH:
Allspice, Almond, Anise, Banana, Blood Orange, Brazil Nut, Cherry, Chestnut, Chile, Cinnamon, Cloves, Coconut, Cranberry, Currant, Date, Fennel, Ginger, Grape, Hazelnut, Lavender, Mandarin, Maple, Mint, Nutmeg, Orange, Passion Fruit, Pear, Pumpkin, Raisin, Strawberry, Vanilla, Walnut
See also White Chocolate

CINNAMON GOES WITH:
Allspice, Almond, Anise, Apple, Banana, Blackberry, Blood Orange, Caramel, Cardamom, Carrot, Cherry, Chile, Chocolate, Coffee, Cranberry, Date, Fig, Ginger, Grape, Mandarin, Mango, Mint, Nutmeg, Orange, Pear, Plum, Pumpkin, Raisin, Raspberry, Vanilla, Walnut

CLOVES GO WITH:
Allspice, Apple, Beet, Cardamom, Carrot, Chocolate, Citrus, Ginger, Nutmeg, Peach, Vanilla

COCONUT GOES WITH:
Allspice, Anise, Banana, Black Pepper, Brazil Nut, Caramel, Cardamom, Chocolate, Citrus, Ginger, Guava, Kiwi Fruit, Mango, Passion Fruit, Pineapple, Rosewater, Vanilla

COFFEE GOES WITH:
Almond, Banana, Chestnut, Cinnamon, Mandarin, Orange

CRANBERRY GOES WITH:
Anise, Apple, Chocolate, Cinnamon, Citrus, Ginger, Mango, Mint, Pear, Rosemary

CURRANT GOES WITH:
Almond, Apple, Cherry, Chocolate, Citrus, Pear, Raspberry

D

DATE GOES WITH:
Almond, Caramel, Cardamom, Chocolate, Cinnamon, Ginger, White Chocolate

DILL GOES WITH:
Anise, Basil, Beet, Carrot, Ginger, Mint

E

ELDERBERRY GOES WITH:
Apricot, Blackberry, Blueberry, Fig, Gooseberry, Honey, Lemon, Mandarin, Mulberry, Peach, Plum, Raspberry, Strawberry

F

FENNEL GOES WITH:
Anise, Cardamom, Chocolate, Watermelon

FIG GOES WITH:
Almond, Anise, Black Pepper, Blood Orange, Blueberry, Cinnamon, Elderberry, Grape, Hazelnut, Honey, Mandarin, Orange, Pear, Vanilla

015

G

GINGER GOES WITH:
Allspice, Almond, Apple, Apricot, Banana, Black Pepper, Blood Orange, Blueberry, Brazil Nut, Caramel, Cardamom, Carrot, Chocolate, Cinnamon, Cloves, Coconut, Cranberry, Date, Dill, Grape, Hazelnut, Lemon, Lime, Lychee, Mandarin, Nutmeg, Orange, Passion Fruit, Peach, Pear, Pineapple, Plum, Raisin, Raspberry, Rhubarb, Vanilla

GOOSEBERRY GOES WITH:
Blackberry, Blueberry, Citrus, Elderberry, Hazelnut, Honey, Lychee, Strawberry, White Chocolate

GRAPE GOES WITH:
Chocolate, Cinnamon, Citrus, Fig, Ginger, Honey, Raisin

GRAPEFRUIT GOES WITH:
Black Pepper, Caramel, Citrus, Mint, Rosemary, Thyme, Tropical Fruit, Vanilla

GUAVA GOES WITH:
Citrus, Coconut, Strawberry, Tropical Fruit

H

HAZELNUT GOES WITH:
Apple, Apricot, Banana, Berries, Caramel, Cherry, Chocolate, Citrus, Fig, Ginger, Gooseberry, Maple, Peach, Pear, Plum

HONEY GOES WITH:
Almond, Apricot, Banana, Beet, Blood Orange, Elderberry, Fig, Gooseberry, Grape, Plum, Raisin, Watermelon

K

KIWI FRUIT GOES WITH:
Apple, Banana, Blackberry, Blueberry, Cherry, Citrus, Coconut, Tropical Fruit

016

L

LAVENDER GOES WITH:
Blueberry, Chocolate, Lemon, Thyme, Vanilla

LEMON GOES WITH:
Apricot, Beet, Blackberry, Black Pepper, Blueberry, Cardamom, Cherry, Citrus, Elderberry, Ginger, Lavender, Mulberry, Nectarine, Peach, Pear, Plum, Raspberry, Strawberry, Tropical Fruit, Watermelon

LIME GOES WITH:
Apple, Berries, Cherry, Ginger, Guava, Papaya, Plum, Strawberry, Watermelon, White Chocolate

LYCHEE GOES WITH:
Citrus, Ginger, Gooseberry, Tropical Fruit, Vanilla

M

MANDARIN GOES WITH:
Apple, Banana, Caramel, Cardamom, Cherry, Chocolate, Cinnamon, Coffee, Elderberry, Fig, Ginger, Hazelnut, Nutmeg, Tropical Fruit

MANGO GOES WITH:
Apple, Banana, Blueberry, Caramel, Cardamom, Chile, Cinnamon, Citrus, Coconut, Cranberry, Kiwi Fruit, Tropical Fruit, Vanilla

MAPLE GOES WITH:
Apple, Carrot, Chocolate, Hazelnut, Pumpkin, Raisin, Vanilla

MINT GOES WITH:
Basil, Beet, Chocolate, Cinnamon, Cranberry, Dill, Grapefruit, Orange, Pomegranate, Strawberry, Thyme

MULBERRY GOES WITH:
Blackberry, Blueberry, Elderberry, Lemon, Orange, Raspberry

N

NECTARINE GOES WITH:
Cherry, Lemon, Raspberry, Rhubarb, Walnut

NUTMEG GOES WITH:
Allspice, Carrot, Chocolate, Cinnamon, Cloves, Ginger, Mandarin, Orange

O

ORANGE GOES WITH:
Almond, Apricot, Basil, Beet, Carrot, Cherry, Chocolate, Cinnamon, Coffee, Cranberry, Fig, Ginger, Grape, Hazelnut, Mint, Mulberry, Nutmeg, Pineapple, Vanilla, Watermelon

P

PAPAYA GOES WITH:
Banana, Berries, Kiwi Fruit, Lime, Mango, Passion Fruit

PASSION FRUIT GOES WITH:
Banana, Chocolate, Coconut, Ginger, Mango, Papaya, Pineapple, Raspberry, Vanilla, White Chocolate

PEACH GOES WITH:
Almond, Anise, Apricot, Blackberry, Cherry, Cloves, Elderberry, Ginger, Hazelnut, Lemon, Raspberry, Rhubarb, Walnut, Watermelon, White Chocolate

PEAR GOES WITH:
Allspice, Almond, Apple, Caramel, Cardamom, Chestnut, Chocolate, Cinnamon, Citrus, Cranberry, Currant, Fig, Ginger, Hazelnut, Vanilla, Walnut

PINEAPPLE GOES WITH:
Coconut, Ginger, Guava, Orange, Passion Fruit

PISTACHIO NUT GOES WITH:
Beet, Rosewater, Watermelon

PLUM GOES WITH:
Almond, Apricot, Blackberry, Black Pepper, Cherry, Chestnut, Cinnamon, Elderberry, Ginger, Hazelnut, Honey, Lemon, Lime, Raspberry, Rhubarb, Vanilla, Walnut, Watermelon

POMEGRANATE GOES WITH:
Anise, Apple, Citrus, Mint, Tropical Fruit, Watermelon

PUMPKIN GOES WITH:
Allspice, Anise, Chocolate, Cinnamon, Citrus, Maple

T

THYME GOES WITH:
Banana, Basil, Carrot, Citrus, Lavender, Mint, Raspberry, Rosemary

V

VANILLA GOES WITH:
Apricot, Brazil Nut, Cherry, Chestnut, Chocolate, Cinnamon, Cloves, Coconut, Fig, Ginger, Grapefruit, Lavender, Lychee, Mango, Maple, Orange, Passion Fruit, Pear, Plum, Raspberry, Strawberry

017

R W

RAISIN GOES WITH:
Carrot, Chocolate, Cinnamon, Citrus, Ginger, Grape, Honey, Maple

WALNUT GOES WITH:
Apple, Apricot, Banana, Caramel, Carrot, Chocolate, Cinnamon, Nectarine, Peach, Pear, Plum

RASPBERRY GOES WITH:
Apricot, Blackberry, Blueberry, Cinnamon, Citrus, Currant, Elderberry, Ginger, Mulberry, Nectarine, Passion Fruit, Peach, Plum, Rhubarb, Thyme, Vanilla, Watermelon

WATERMELON GOES WITH:
Blackberry, Blueberry, Chile, Fennel, Honey, Lemon, Lime, Orange, Peach, Pistachio Nut, Plum, Pomegranate, Raspberry, Strawberry

RHUBARB GOES WITH:
Apple, Apricot, Blackberry, Black Pepper, Blueberry, Citrus, Ginger, Nectarine, Peach, Plum, Raspberry, Strawberry

WHITE CHOCOLATE GOES WITH:
Cherry, Date, Gooseberry, Lime, Passion Fruit, Peach, Strawberry

ROSEMARY GOES WITH:
Apple, Basil, Citrus, Cranberry, Thyme

ROSEWATER GOES WITH:
Almond, Cardamom, Coconut, Pistachio Nut

S

STRAWBERRY GOES WITH:
Apple, Blackberry, Black Pepper, Blueberry, Chocolate, Elderberry, Gooseberry, Guava, Lemon, Lime, Mint, Rhubarb, Vanilla, Watermelon, White Chocolate

PART

01

THE CAKES

The Queens

HERE ARE MY QUEENS! The cakes in this section are my absolute favorites and, in my opinion, they are all more than worthy of the royal title. They are the showstoppers and party girls that love attention. They make a grand centerpiece for your table or event, creating a mood and setting the scene with ease and style. These queens are the core of the book and demonstrate just what you can achieve when you unleash the artist within and bring together the base cakes, fillings, frostings, and sweet finishes. Think outside the box and enjoy dreaming up your own majestic creations.

022

023

024

coconut & limoncello cake

WITH HONEY BUTTERCREAM & LEMON CURD

Visually speaking, this delightful cake is my favorite. It has an air of sophistication and simply oozes style. It has a coconut cake base, which is beautifully teamed with lemon liqueur, lemon curd, and notes of vanilla and honey.

026

**MAKES ONE 2-TIERED
8-INCH ROUND CAKE**

1 batch Honey Buttercream
(page 113)

1 batch Lemon Curd (page 133)

2 x Coconut Cake (page 85)

1 batch Limoncello Glaze
(page 129)

TO CROWN

lightly toasted coconut flakes

large lemon-yellow or cream
organic rose petals

small corkscrew willow twigs,
about 4 inches long

1–2 organic
elderflower blossom sprigs

I'M A BIG FAN OF
ELDERFLOWER. I LOVE
ITS DELICATE AND
EXQUISITE CLUSTERS OF
PETITE FLOWERS AND
BERRIES, AS WELL AS ITS
SUBTLE, FRESH SCENT.
IT'S ALLURING AND
OH-SO-GRACEFUL.

027

Prepare the honey buttercream, following the instructions on page 113.

Prepare the lemon curd, following the instructions on page 133.

Prepare two coconut cakes, following the instructions on page 85.

While the cakes are cooling, prepare the limoncello glaze, following the instructions on page 129. Pour the limoncello glaze evenly over the top of the cooled cakes and let stand until set.

To assemble, place one of the cakes on a cake stand or serving plate. Using a clean, damp spatula, spread half the honey buttercream over the top of the cake. Place the second cake on top and spread the remaining buttercream over the top of the second cake. Use some of the buttercream oozing out of the layers to thinly "whitewash" the sides (see page 101).

Just before serving, spoon the lemon curd over the top of the cake, allowing some to drizzle down the sides.

Cover the lemon curd with coconut flakes, piling them a little higher in the center and allowing them to spill slightly over the side of the cake, into the drizzling lemon curd.

Pile several large rose petals in the center of the cake. Place the willow twigs on top of the petals and tuck some underneath. Finally, place the elderflower blossoms in and around the rose petals.

COCONUT & LIMONCELLO CAKE

028

watermelon cake
WITH SWEET COCONUT CREAM, FIGS & BERRIES

I am in love with this cake. It's so refreshing and makes a healthy alternative to a traditional celebration cake. It's perfect for a summer party – and there's no feeling guilty about going back for seconds. What's more, it looks spectacular! The dairy-free coconut cream adds a touch of decadence and comfort.

MAKES ONE CAKE (SIZE DEPENDS ON DIAMETER OF WATERMELON)

1 whole 11-lb seedless
ripe watermelon (see Note)

1 batch Dairy-Free Sweet
Coconut Cream (page 131)

TO CROWN

about 8 oz strawberries

2–3 figs, halved

handful of raspberries

a few pomegranate seeds

jasmine vine

031

Place the watermelon on a large chopping board. (This is going to get a little messy!) Prevent your board from slipping during cutting by placing a damp cloth underneath it. Slice the top and bottom off the melon to create a flat top and base.

With the melon standing on one end, remove the rind, including the hard white flesh. (I find it easiest to cut into the melon along the white edge where the rind meets the pink fruit and cut out the circle that will be the "cake.") If your cutting is a little irregular, just trim the watermelon cake to achieve a uniform, cylindrical shape, or as close as you can manage. Alternatively, you may like to cut the rind off in sections and trim to achieve the same cylindrical appearance. Pat the cake dry with a paper towel, place it on a cake stand or serving plate, and set aside.

Prepare the coconut cream, following the instructions on page 131. This can be used as a topping, or you can do as I do and serve it on the side so guests can dollop as much as they desire on their fresh fruit. If using it as a topping, just smooth it over the surface of the melon, but do make sure you pat the watermelon dry first, so the cream doesn't slide off.

Cut some of the strawberries in half lengthwise. I love to keep the leaves attached for visual appeal — a little extra greenery looks so fresh. Pile on a few whole strawberries to make a sturdy layer. Now add the fig halves — they look best face-up and on a slight angle. Fill any gaps with strawberry halves, raspberries, and a sprinkling of pomegranate seeds. Refrigerate until ready to serve. Just before serving you could scatter on a few jasmine blooms if you like, but I love the trailing nature of this plant, so just a little around the base of the cake also adds a pretty touch.

NOTE: I USED AN 11-POUND WATERMELON, WHICH WOULD SERVE ABOUT 12 PEOPLE, BUT FEEL FREE TO USE A LARGER OR SMALLER MELON TO SUIT THE NUMBER OF GUESTS.

WATERMELON CAKE

032

lemon & rosemary cake

WITH VANILLA BUTTERCREAM

This is my favorite cake, flavor-wise. I've always loved lemon and rosemary cookies, so I wanted to try a cake with these unexpected flavors. The burst of citrus is grounded by the subtlety of the rosemary. Tender, sweet, and tangy, this bold cake will awaken the taste buds.

MAKES ONE 2-TIERED
8-INCH ROUND CAKE

1 batch Vanilla Buttercream
(page 112)

2 x Lemonade Cake (page 83;
see variation in the method)

2–3 tablespoons finely chopped
fresh rosemary or 2 teaspoons
dried rosemary

½ cup (3¾ oz) superfine sugar

¼ cup freshly squeezed and strained
lemon juice

TO CROWN
long fresh rosemary sprigs

3 organic yellow and green
ornamental kale flowers (it's unlikely
you would eat these, but you could!)

1–2 elderflower sprigs

035

Prepare the vanilla buttercream, following the instructions on page 112.

Prepare two lemonade cakes, following the instructions on page 83, but add rosemary to the batter when adding the vanilla and zest.

While the cakes are cooking, place the sugar and lemon juice in a saucepan and stir over low heat until the sugar dissolves. Remove from the heat and set aside to cool.

Remove the cakes from the oven and use a skewer to prick the cakes all over, then leave them to stand in the pans for 10 minutes.

Pour the cooled syrup over the cakes and then leave them to stand until completely cool.

To assemble, place one of the cakes on a stand or serving plate and, using a clean, damp spatula, spread with half the vanilla buttercream. Place the other cake on top, spread the top with buttercream, then use some of the buttercream oozing out of the layers to thinly whitewash the sides (see page 101). Take your rosemary sprigs and place them around the base of the cake. Place two kale flowers on top of the cake – it would look best if you chose one slightly smaller than the other. (You can remove a few outer leaves from one to achieve this.) You don't want to crowd the kale flowers, or it will make the cake top-heavy. Now place one smaller kale flower on the right side at the base of the cake. A small elderflower sprig adds a delicate touch of softness.

GET AHEAD
THIS CAKE CAN BE MADE IN ADVANCE. THE KALE FLOWERS ARE HARDY AND WILL HOLD UP WELL IN THE REFRIGERATOR. THEREFORE, THIS CAKE WOULD BE A GOOD CHOICE FOR A WEDDING CAKE THAT WILL BE LEFT ON DISPLAY FOR SOME TIME.

LEMON & ROSEMARY CAKE

036

cardamom cake

WITH SPICED SYRUP & CANDIED ORANGES

This gorgeous cake smells just like the festive season. It's a single-tiered cake, so it couldn't be easier to assemble. I don't think this cake needs any buttercream or frosting; it's satisfying enough just soaked with spiced syrup and covered in candied orange slices. A dollop of fresh cream would make a nice addition.

038

SUITABLE FOR... A WONDERFUL CAKE FOR AN INDIAN DINNER PARTY, OR TO SPICE UP A SPECIAL ANNIVERSARY. IT WOULD ALSO BE A GREAT CHOICE FOR GUESTS WHO PREFER A CAKE THAT'S NOT TOO SWEET.

039

MAKES ONE 9-INCH ROUND CAKE

1 x Cardamom Cake (page 90)

1 batch Spiced Syrup (page 136)

TO CROWN

2 batches Candied Orange Slices (page 149)

Prepare the cardamom cake, following the instructions on page 90.

Prepare the spiced syrup, following the instructions on page 136.

Prepare two batches of candied orange slices, following the instructions on page 149.

When the cake is cool, transfer to a stand or serving plate and prick the cake all over with a skewer. Drizzle the spiced syrup all over the cake, starting in the center. Let the syrup drip down the sides to make it look even more luscious.

Start placing the candied orange slices in a circle around the edge of the cake, each one slightly overlapping the next. Then place a circle inside that one, with those slices slightly overlapping each other as well as the first circle.

CARDAMOM CAKE

040

vanilla cake

WITH ROSE BUTTERCREAM

This three-tiered mini vanilla cake is sweet in every sense. Ideal for small parties or as a generous dinner party dessert for four, it also makes a gorgeous gift. The delicate floral flavors of vanilla and rose work beautifully together.

042

MAKES ONE 3-TIERED
6-INCH CAKE

1 batch Rose Buttercream
(page 118)

2 batches Vanilla Cake
batter (page 82)

TO CROWN

edible organic pink or coral roses

edible leaves

043

Prepare the rose buttercream, following the instructions on page 118.

Prepare two batches of vanilla cake batter, following the instructions on page 82. This mixture will make enough for three 6-inch cakes.

Grease three 6-inch cake pans. Pour a third of the batter into each pan. Cook the cakes following the instructions on page 82, but cook for 25–30 minutes. Let cakes cool completely.

To assemble, place one of the cakes on a stand or serving plate. Using a clean, damp spatula, spread one-third of the buttercream over the top, then repeat with the second cake and another third of the buttercream. Now invert the third and final layer and place it on top – this will give you a lovely smooth top to work with. Smooth over the remaining buttercream and use some of the buttercream oozing out of the layers to lightly "whitewash" the sides (see page 101). Crown with the roses and edible leaves.

THIS CUTE LITTLE
CAKE LOOKS GREAT
ON A MINIATURE
CAKE PEDESTAL.

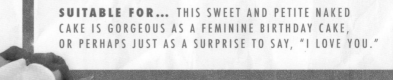

SUITABLE FOR... THIS SWEET AND PETITE NAKED CAKE IS GORGEOUS AS A FEMININE BIRTHDAY CAKE, OR PERHAPS JUST AS A SURPRISE TO SAY, "I LOVE YOU."

VANILLA CAKE

044

layered crêpe cake

WITH WATERMELON & ROSE JAM, CHANTILLY CREAM & BERRIES

The best thing about this little gem of a recipe is its simplicity. There is nothing really precise about it – it's just layer upon layer upon layer of deliciousness. You can't go wrong.

SUITABLE FOR... THIS MAKES A FANTASTIC OPTION FOR A BIRTHDAY BREAKFAST-IN-BED, A LOVELY REWARD CAKE, OR A SHOWSTOPPER FOR A DINNER PARTY.

MAKES ONE 8-INCH LAYERED CRÊPE CAKE

047

1 batch Watermelon and Rose Jam (page 148)

1 batch Chantilly Cream (page 130)

1 x Crêpe Stack (page 95)

TO CROWN
fresh raspberries, yellow nasturtiums, roses, baby arugula leaves, jasmine flowers

Prepare the watermelon and rose jam, following the instructions on page 148.

Prepare the chantilly cream, following the instructions on page 130.

Prepare the crêpe stack, following the instructions on page 95.

To assemble the crêpe cake, place one crêpe on a stand or serving plate and smear 1 heaping tablespoon of the jam over it, spreading it right to the edges. Spread with a layer of chantilly cream. Top with another crêpe and repeat the process until all the crêpes have been used. When you get to the last crêpe, spoon a few tablespoons of jam onto the center, top with the remaining chantilly cream and the berries, and arrange the flowers and leaves on top.

048

almond & lemon cake

WITH LEMON BUTTERCREAM

It's hard to stop at one slice of this cake, so a two-tiered version makes sense to me – it's just heavenly! I find that this cake appeals to most tastes, and it's suitable for just about any occasion.

MAKES ONE 2-TIERED
8-INCH ROUND CAKE

2 x Almond Cake (page 84)

1 batch Citrus Buttercream
(page 120), made with lemon juice

TO CROWN

organic edible roses in shades of
orange, cream, bright yellow and
coral, plus a few rosebuds

a length of green vine,
about 16 inches

a few eucalyptus seed pods

eucalyptus leaves, or similar

I LOVE THE EARTHY
COMBINATION OF ALMOND
AND LEMON. IT HAS A
WONDERFUL DEPTH
OF FLAVOR AND IS
ZINGY AND MOREISH.

051

Prepare two almond cakes, following the
instructions on page 84.

Prepare the citrus buttercream, following the
instructions on page 120, using lemon juice.

To assemble, place one cake on a stand or serving
plate (I show it here on a round wooden board, resting
on a vintage metal sieve) and spread with half the
lemon buttercream. Top with the second cake, then
spread the top with the remaining buttercream. Use
a little of the cream oozing out of the layers to lightly
whitewash the side of the cake (see page 101).

Crown with your chosen roses – a few rosebuds
placed in the gaps between the larger blooms
gives a more balanced and finished look.

Decorate the base of the cake with a length of
vine entwined around it and place seed pods
and eucalyptus leaves on the side.

ALMOND & LEMON CAKE

052

orange yogurt cake

WITH ORANGE SYRUP & MASCARPONE BUTTERCREAM

Here's a mouthwatering cake with a delightful orange aroma, soaked in sweet syrup. It's moist and lush and you'll find it hard to stop at one slice. It's definitely a crowd-pleaser.

MAKES ONE 4-TIERED
8½-INCH CAKE

4 x Orange Yogurt Cake
(page 81)

1 batch Mascarpone
Buttercream (page 112)

1 batch Orange Syrup
(page 137)

TO CROWN
edible organic peach roses

succulent leaves, such as jade
(see Note)

12-inch jasmine vine

Prepare four orange yogurt cakes, following
the instructions on page 81.

Prepare the mascarpone buttercream, following
the instructions on page 112.

Prepare the orange syrup, following the instructions
on page 137.

When the cakes have cooled slightly, prick holes
all over them with a skewer, then pour a quarter
of the hot syrup over each cake and leave to
cool completely.

To assemble, place one of the cakes on a stand
or serving plate and spread with a quarter of the
buttercream. Repeat with the remaining cakes and
buttercream, finishing with a layer of buttercream.
Use some of the buttercream oozing out of the layers
to lightly whitewash the sides (see page 101).

Crown with roses – here I chose a large bloom and
a few small delicate buds. I placed the large bloom
on top of the cake on its side, and the smaller blooms
alongside it. A few strategically placed pieces
of jade add some green and texture and a feeling
of the exotic. Trail your jasmine vine at the base of
the cake. A few dropped rose petals look lovely, too.

055

NOTE: SUCCULENTS, WITH THEIR HARDY FLESH AND WOODY
STEMS, ARE DECORATIVE, BUT BE CAREFUL NOT TO PLACE THE
CUT STEMS ON YOUR CAKE WHERE THE SAP CAN DRIP INTO THE
CREAMS – IT WILL NOT TASTE GOOD! THEY SHOULD BE CLEANED
AND DRIED BEFORE USE. RINSE THEM IN WATER AND PAT DRY
WITH A KITCHEN TOWEL, THEN WRAP THE WOODY STEMS IN FOIL
OR FLORAL TAPE.

ORANGE YOGURT CAKE

056

chocolate cake

WITH CHANTILLY CREAM & FRUIT

There's just something about a tiered chocolate cake, isn't there? When I was young, my mother would always let us choose whichever type of cake we would like to celebrate our birthday, and chocolate cake was always at the top of my wish list. I have passed this tradition down to my family, and chocolate is always at the top of my son Sam's wish list too. This recipe is super-easy. It might look decadent, but it's actually not too rich. It also has real "wow" factor when you grace the table with its beauty.

058

MAKES ONE 4-TIERED 8-INCH CAKE

2 x Chocolate Cake (page 86)

2 batches Chantilly Cream (page 130)

TO CROWN

about 8 oz small strawberries, some not hulled

handful of raspberries

handful of blueberries

handful of pomegranate seeds

059

Prepare two chocolate cakes following the instructions on page 86. When cool, use a large serrated knife to cut each cake in half horizontally, to give four layers in total.

Prepare the chantilly cream, following the instructions on page 130.

To assemble, place one of the cake layers on a cake stand or serving plate and spread with a quarter of the chantilly cream, leaving a ¾- to 1¼-inch border, to allow for spreading when you place another layer on top. Repeat this process with the remaining layers and cream. When you get to the last layer, use the remaining cream to top the cake.

Halve about four or five strawberries. Place the whole strawberries around the periphery of the cake, then start to fill to the center. Scatter the halved strawberries around the top of the cake. Repeat with the raspberries. Finish with a scattering of blueberries and pomegranate seeds.

TO MAKE THIS CAKE LOOK LUSH AND ABUNDANT, EVERY QUADRANT OF THE TOP OF THE CAKE NEEDS TO HAVE A LITTLE OF ALL OF THE INGREDIENTS. IT'S ABOUT BALANCE.

060

cheese wheel cake

WITH FRESH & DRIED FRUIT

Not a baker? Well, I've got you covered! With this cake, all you need to do is buy the cheeses, then stack and decorate them; you could have up to five tiers. Choose one style of cheese or a mix of different cheeses with different colored rinds for interest and effect. You could opt for a miniature version or a magnificent large cheese wheel elevated on a beautiful pedestal.

062

SUITABLE FOR... A WEDDING, A LARGE CORPORATE PARTY, A SOPHISTICATED AFFAIR FOR CHEESE-LOVERS, OR FOR GUESTS WHO DON'T HAVE A SWEET TOOTH.

As many cheese wheels as you want layers – each wheel has to be around 1 inch larger or smaller than the cheese on top of or below it (see Note)

TO CROWN

4-inch length of green vine

pansies

pale pink organic roses

pink chive flowers

basil flowers

TO SERVE

crackers

dried fruit, such as apricots or muscatel raisins

fresh fruit, such as grapes, red currants, or stone fruit

063

Tier your wheels of cheese – arrange the hardest and largest cheeses on the bottom to help support the weight of the others on top. A heavy base or cake stand will make for easy transportation and add visual interest. (I have placed this cheese stack on a rustic slab of tree trunk – it weighs a ton, but looks amazing!)

Place your chosen vine at the base of your wheel cake – this is decorative but not edible. Crown the top of the cake with leaves and flowers, and place them randomly on the tiers.

Have plenty of cheese knives and plates on hand. Your guests can help themselves, or you can serve small plates of cheese wedges to share with drinks. Serve with a couple of cocktails to suit your event and menu – take cues from your cheeses – or you may like to serve wine. Riesling or Gewürztraminer work well with cheese. If you prefer a red, opt for a Pinot Noir, as heavy red wines can overpower cheese.

NOTE: SOFT CHEESES AREN'T SAFE FOR PREGNANT WOMEN TO CONSUME, SO USE A FEW VARIETIES IN CASE ANY OF YOUR GUESTS ARE EXPECTING.

CHEESE WHEEL CAKE

064

meringue stack

WITH HAZELNUT LIQUEUR CREAM, FIGS & MAPLE SYRUP

Here is another unconventional yet delectable "cake." Aim for simple, fresh flavors to accompany the meringue, and keep it to only two tiers.

067

MAKES ONE 2-TIERED
7-INCH MERINGUE STACK

2 x Meringue Stack (page 94)

1 batch Chantilly Cream
(page 130)

2–3 tablespoons hazelnut liqueur,
such as Frangelico

TO CROWN

5 fresh figs, halved, or
Caramelized Figs (page 153)

pure maple syrup to drizzle

Prepare two meringue stacks, following the
instructions on page 94.

Prepare the chantilly cream, following the instructions
on page 130. Fold the hazelnut liqueur into the
chantilly cream.

To assemble, place one meringue stack on a cake
stand or serving plate. (You may like to gently crush
the meringue for ease of layering, but don't be too
heavy-handed or you will end up with an Eton mess!)
Spread the meringue with half the cream. Top with
the remaining meringue stack and spread over the
remaining cream. Top with the fig halves. Drizzle with
pure maple syrup to finish.

GET AHEAD
YOU CAN STORE THE
COOKED MERINGUE IN
AN AIRTIGHT CONTAINER
FOR UP TO 2 DAYS.
DO NOT REFRIGERATE.

SUITABLE FOR... MORNING TEA ON A LOVED ONE'S
BIRTHDAY, OR A SPECTACULAR FINISH TO A SUMMER
DINNER PARTY.

MERINGUE STACK

068

chocolate cake

WITH SALTED CARAMEL POPCORN, CHOCOLATE FUDGE FROSTING & DARK CHOCOLATE GLAZE

This cake is all about decadence and abundance and will really impress. It's a chocoholic's dream and is pure, gooey goodness. It can be made gluten-free by using gluten-free self-rising flour instead of wheat flour in the chocolate cake recipe.

070

SUITABLE FOR... THIS IS A FUN AND PLAYFUL CAKE, IDEAL FOR AN OLDER CHILD'S BIRTHDAY PARTY, OR FOR AN ADULT WHO IS STILL A CHILD AT HEART.

MAKES ONE 3-TIERED
8-INCH ROUND CAKE

2 batches Chocolate Fudge Frosting
(page 128)

3 x Chocolate Cake (page 86)

1 batch Dark Chocolate Glaze
(page 128)

TO CROWN

1 batch Salted Caramel Popcorn
(page 142)

Prepare two batches of the chocolate fudge frosting, following the instructions on page 128.

Prepare three chocolate cakes, following the instructions on page 86.

While the cakes are cooling, prepare the chocolate glaze, following the instructions on page 128.

Prepare the salted caramel popcorn, following the instructions on page 142.

To assemble, place one of the chocolate cakes on a stand or serving plate and spread with a third of the chocolate fudge frosting. Repeat this process with the remaining cakes and frosting.

Cover the top layer with the salted caramel popcorn, piling it higher in the center of the cake.

Drizzle the cake generously with the dark chocolate glaze, allowing the sauce to drizzle down the sides of the cake.

CHOCOLATE CAKE

072

lychee cake

WITH MASCARPONE BUTTERCREAM

The lightly floral taste of lychees brings an exotic touch to this magnificent cake. Unleash your creativity by topping it with a delicate garland of handmade pom-poms.

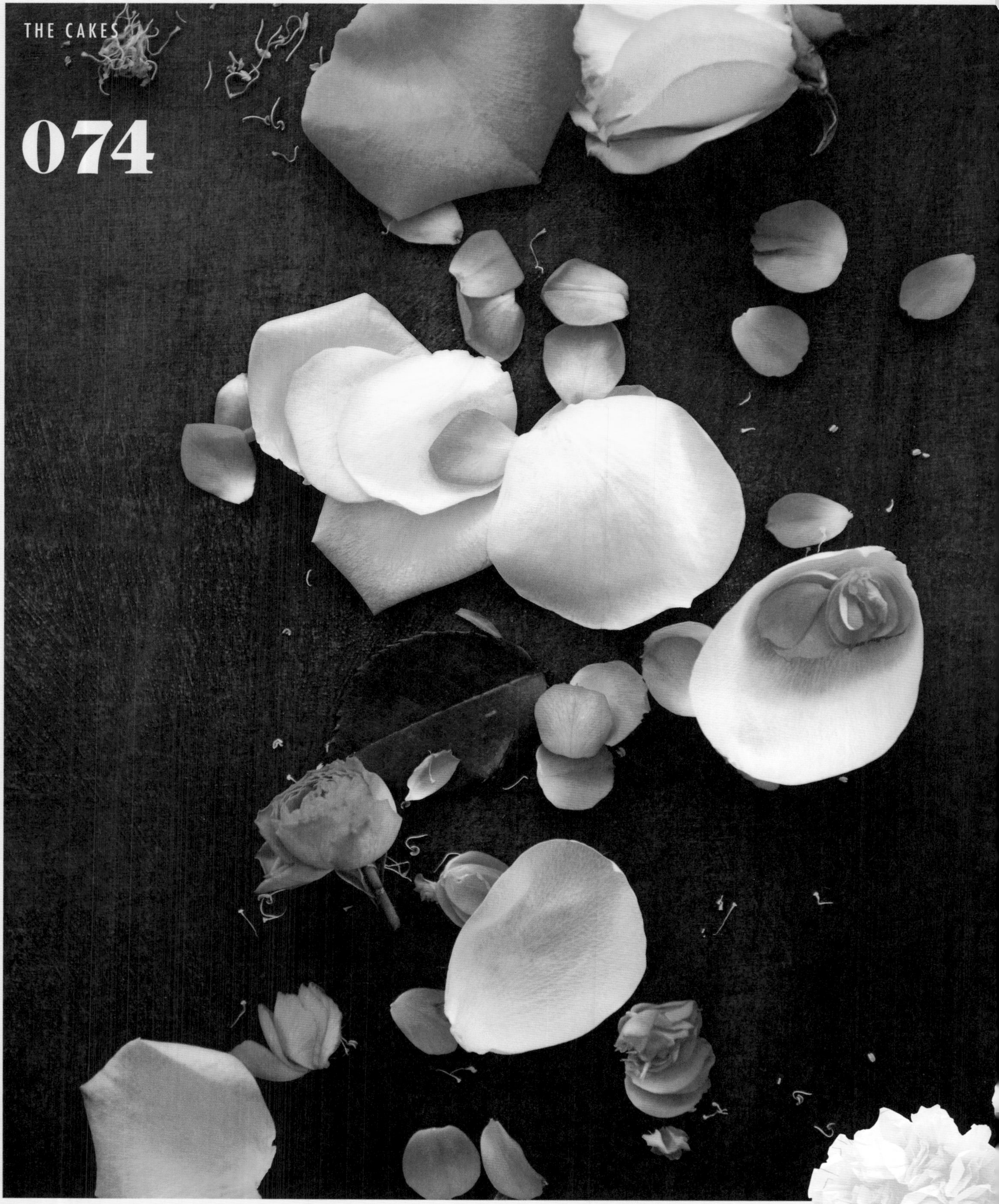

MAKES ONE 2-TIERED
8-INCH ROUND CAKE

1 batch Mascarpone Buttercream
(page 112)

2 x Lychee Cake (page 91)

TO CROWN

pom-pom garland cake
topper (page 221)

fuchsias, miniature edible organic
roses, and/or impatiens

HERE I USE A VINTAGE
WOODEN DRUM SIEVE AS
A CAKE STAND. IT WAS A
GREAT FIND AT MY LOCAL
ANTIQUES STORE.

075

Prepare the mascarpone buttercream, following
the instructions on page 112.

Prepare two lychee cakes, following the instructions
on page 91.

To assemble, place one of the cakes on a stand
or serving plate. Spread the cake with half the
mascarpone buttercream. Top with the second cake
and spread the top with the remaining buttercream.
Use a little of the cream oozing from between the
layers to lightly the sides (see page 101).

Crown the cake with a mixture of your chosen
flowers. Place the tiniest blooms around the edge
of the cake top and at the base of the cake,
otherwise they will get lost. If you use a slightly
larger plate, then you could add some larger
blooms, randomly scattered at the base of the cake.

Top the cake with a homemade pom-pom garland
cake topper for a little fun.

Bases to inspire

MEET MY BASE CAKES – they could be the foundation of your next delicious cake! I've included quite a variety of flavors here. Along with childhood favorites and popular choices for weddings and parties, there are also a few unusual ones just to keep things interesting. In addition, for the health-conscious there are some gluten-free and flourless recipes, so there really is something for everyone here. For flavor-matching inspiration, explore my "this goes with that" chart on page 12, to help you pair the cakes with the fillings and frostings and the sweet finishes.

THE CAKES

078

079

080

I think it could be said that the Victoria sponge is one of the most classic of base cakes. This fête favorite is full of charm, and I invite you to try any manner of flavor combinations, which will help transform this cake's somewhat dull reputation into something truly amazing. However, whatever you try, chantilly cream simply must be involved!

victoria sponge

GREAT FLAVOR COMBINATIONS...

CHANTILLY CREAM (PAGE 130), ABUNDANT FRESH STRAWBERRIES (SOME WHOLE, SOME HALVED), AND A LIGHT DUSTING OF POWDERED SUGAR. DECORATE WITH SOME DELICATE STRAWBERRY BLOOMS.

CHANTILLY CREAM (PAGE 130), BALSAMIC CHERRIES (PAGE 152), AND A GENEROUS SERVING OF DARK CHOCOLATE GLAZE (PAGE 128) ON THE SIDE.

CHANTILLY CREAM (PAGE 130), BUTTERSCOTCH BUTTERCREAM (PAGE 114), AND APPLE COMPOTE (PAGE 144). WARNING – THIS MAY RESULT IN A WAR OF SPOONS!

MAKES ONE 8-INCH ROUND CAKE

7 tablespoons unsalted butter, softened, plus extra for greasing

½ cup (3½ oz) superfine sugar

⅞ cup (3½ oz) self-rising flour

1 teaspoon baking powder

2 eggs, lightly beaten

Preheat the oven to 350°F. Lightly grease an 8-inch round cake pan.

Using an electric mixer, beat the butter and sugar until light and fluffy.

In a medium bowl, combine the flour and baking powder. In alternate batches, gradually add the beaten eggs and the flour mixture to the butter and sugar mixture, beating well after each addition.

Pour the batter into the prepared pan and bake for 20 minutes, or until a skewer inserted into the center of the cake comes out clean. Let the cake stand in the pan for 10 minutes, then turn out and transfer to a wire rack to cool completely.

orange yogurt cake

The orange flavor of this cake is to die for, and the clever addition of yogurt adds moisture. This cake can also be made using gluten-free flour if you are on a special diet.

MAKES ONE 8½-INCH ROUND CAKE

4 cups (1 lb) all-purpose or gluten-free flour

4 teaspoons baking soda

pinch of salt

1 cup (9¼ oz) plain Greek-style yogurt

zest and juice of 1 orange

1 teaspoon vanilla bean paste or natural vanilla extract

1¼ cups (20 tablespoons) unsalted butter, softened, plus extra for greasing

1½ cups (10½ oz) superfine sugar

3 eggs, lightly beaten

Preheat the oven to 350°F. Lightly grease an 8½-inch round cake pan.

Sift the flour, baking soda, and salt into a bowl and use a whisk to combine well.

Place the yogurt, orange zest and juice, and vanilla in another bowl and whisk to combine well.

Using an electric mixer, beat the butter and sugar until light and fluffy. Gradually add the yogurt mixture, alternating with the flour mixture and the beaten egg, and beat until well combined.

Pour the batter into the prepared pan, smooth the top, and bake for 45–50 minutes, or until a skewer inserted into the center of the cake comes out clean. Let the cake stand in the pan for 10 minutes, then turn out and transfer to a wire rack to cool completely.

GREAT FLAVOR COMBINATIONS...
CITRUS BUTTERCREAM (PAGE 120) AND A CONFETTI OF MARIGOLD PETALS MAKE FOR A CHEERY WINTER TREAT. THIS CAKE IS BOUND TO BRIGHTEN ANYONE'S DAY.

RICH CHOCOLATE BUTTERCREAM (PAGE 121) WITH SOME SHAVED DARK CHOCOLATE — A MATCH MADE IN HEAVEN.

082

This recipe is extremely versatile. You can use just about any filling or frosting with it. You can also make the tiers smaller or larger using various quantities of the same batter in different pans — however, work out how much the bowl of your electric mixer can accommodate before attempting to double the quantity.

vanilla cake

MAKES ONE 8-INCH ROUND CAKE

1½ cups (6¼ oz) all-purpose flour

2 teaspoons baking powder

¼ teaspoon salt

½ cup (8 tablespoons) unsalted butter, softened, plus extra for greasing

1 cup (7¾ oz) superfine sugar

4 eggs, separated

½ teaspoon vanilla bean paste or natural vanilla extract

½ cup milk

GREAT FLAVOR COMBINATIONS...
ELDERFLOWER BUTTERCREAM (PAGE 124) WITH FRESH HALVED STRAWBERRIES AND ELDERFLOWER SPRIGS TO DECORATE.

BLACK CHERRY AND VANILLA BUTTERCREAM (PAGE 120) WITH BALSAMIC CHERRIES (PAGE 152). THIS IS RUSTIC BUT VERY LUSH.

CHANTILLY CREAM (PAGE 130), RASPBERRY AND ROSE BUTTERCREAM (PAGE 118) WITH FRESH AND PERKY RASPBERRIES, AND A SCATTERING OF PINK AND/OR RED ROSE PETALS. ANY GIRLY GIRL WOULD LOVE THIS. IT LOOKS AND TASTES PRETTY.

Preheat the oven to 325°F. Lightly grease an 8-inch round cake pan.

Sift the flour, baking powder, and salt into a large bowl and combine well with a whisk.

Using an electric mixer, beat the butter and sugar until light and fluffy. Add the egg yolks one at a time, beating until well combined and scraping down the sides of the bowl from time to time. Add the vanilla and beat until well combined. With the mixer on low speed, gradually add the flour mixture and milk in alternate batches, beating until well combined.

Place the egg whites in another clean bowl. Using an electric mixer, beat the egg whites until stiff peaks form. Fold one-third of the egg whites into the batter to loosen, then gently fold in the remaining egg whites. Be gentle and patient in this process, as you want to keep as much air in the batter as possible to keep the cake light.

Pour the batter into the prepared pan and bake for 20–30 minutes, or until a skewer inserted into the center of the cake comes out clean. Let the cake stand in the pan for 10 minutes, then turn out and transfer to a wire rack to cool completely.

lemonade cake

This is one of my favorite bases. Tender, sweet, and tangy, this bold lemon cake will brighten anyone's day. The flavor dances on your tongue, a little like lemonade.

MAKES ONE 8-INCH ROUND CAKE

1½ cups (6¼ oz) all-purpose flour

¼ teaspoon baking powder

¼ teaspoon baking soda

½ cup (8 tablespoons) unsalted butter, softened, plus extra for greasing

1 cup (7¾ oz) superfine sugar or stevia (see Note)

2 eggs, at room temperature

1 teaspoon vanilla bean paste or natural vanilla extract

zest of 1 lemon

½ teaspoon salt

½ cup (4½ oz) plain Greek-style yogurt, at room temperature

¼ cup strained lemon juice

083

Preheat the oven to 325°F. Lightly grease an 8-inch round cake pan.

Sift the flour, baking powder, and baking soda into a large bowl and use a whisk to combine well.

Using an electric mixer, beat the butter and sugar until light and fluffy. Add the eggs one at a time, beating well after each addition, scraping down the sides of the bowl occasionally. Add the vanilla, lemon zest, and salt and beat until just combined. With the mixer on low speed, add the flour mixture and yogurt in alternate batches and beat until just combined. Do not overbeat. Add the lemon juice and mix until just combined.

Pour the batter into the prepared pan and smooth the top. Bake for 40–45 minutes, or until the cake is golden and a skewer inserted into the center comes out clean. Let the cake stand in the pan for 10 minutes, then turn out and transfer to a wire rack to cool completely.

NOTE: If using stevia, make sure you use a brand that replaces the sugar with an equal amount of stevia. Some brands use a considerably smaller quantity of stevia and this will adversely affect the batter, so make sure you check the packet.

GREAT FLAVOR COMBINATIONS...
MASCARPONE BUTTERCREAM (PAGE 112), FRESH STRAWBERRIES, A DUSTING OF POWDERED SUGAR, AND A FEW RANDOMLY PLACED STRAWBERRY BLOOMS. HAVE SOME FRIENDS OVER FOR MORNING TEA — THEY WILL WANT TO LINGER IF A SECOND HELPING MIGHT BE IN THE CARDS!

084

This is a scrumptious cake that goes well with many other flavors. While it is a good fit for any season, I think it's perfect for serving at an event held in a sunny spring or summer garden. It's an ideal base cake to get creative with.

almond cake

MAKES ONE 8-INCH ROUND CAKE

1½ cups (6¼ oz) all-purpose flour

1 teaspoon baking powder

½ teaspoon baking soda

½ teaspoon salt

½ cup (1¾ oz) almond meal

½ cup (8 tablespoons) unsalted butter, softened, plus extra for greasing

1 cup (7¾ oz) superfine sugar

zest of 1 small lemon

1½ teaspoons almond extract

2 eggs, at room temperature

1 cup (8½ oz) sour cream

GREAT FLAVOR COMBINATIONS...
CINNAMON BUTTERCREAM (PAGE 114) AND CRUSHED PRALINE (PAGE 147). THE CINNAMON ADDS SPICE, WHILE THE PRALINE DELIVERS CRUNCH AND ANOTHER LAYER OF SWEETNESS.

Preheat the oven to 325°F. Lightly grease an 8-inch round cake pan.

Sift the flour, baking powder, baking soda, and salt into a large bowl. Add the almond meal and use a whisk to combine well.

Using an electric mixer, beat the butter, sugar, lemon zest, and almond extract until light and fluffy. Add the eggs one at a time, beating well after each addition. With the motor on low speed, add the flour mixture and sour cream alternately in small batches and beat until well combined.

Pour the batter into the prepared pan and bake for 40–50 minutes, or until a skewer inserted into the center of the cake comes out clean. Let the cake stand in the pan for 10 minutes, then turn out and transfer to a wire rack to cool completely.

coconut cake

The coconut flavor of this lovely moist cake is setting trends and pleasing crowds everywhere. It's a wonderful choice for summer events, and pairs effortlessly with fresh fruit – especially tropical fruit.

MAKES ONE 8-INCH ROUND CAKE

2½ cups (10 oz) all-purpose or gluten-free flour

2 teaspoons baking powder

¾ teaspoon salt

5 large egg whites

1 large egg

1 cup coconut cream

1 teaspoon vanilla bean paste or natural vanilla extract

1 teaspoon coconut extract

¾ cup (12 tablespoons) unsalted butter, softened, plus extra for greasing

1 cup (7¾ oz) superfine sugar or stevia (see Notes)

Preheat the oven to 325°F. Lightly grease an 8-inch round cake pan.

Sift the flour, baking powder and salt into a bowl and use a whisk to combine well.

Using a fork, lightly beat the egg whites and the egg in a bowl, then add the coconut cream, vanilla and coconut extract and whisk until well combined.

Using an electric mixer, beat the butter and sugar until light and fluffy. With the mixer on low speed, gradually add the flour mixture and the egg mixture in alternate batches and beat until well combined.

Spoon the batter into the prepared pan and smooth the top. Bake for 20–30 minutes, or until a skewer inserted into the center of the cake comes out clean. Let the cake stand in the pan for 10 minutes, then turn out and transfer to a wire rack to cool completely.

NOTES: If using stevia, make sure you use a brand that replaces sugar with an equal amount of stevia. Some brands use a considerably smaller quantity of stevia and this will adversely affect the batter, so make sure you check the packet.

If you prefer, you can make two thinner cakes by dividing the batter between two 8-inch cake pans and reducing the cooking time to 15–20 minutes.

GREAT FLAVOR COMBINATIONS...

PASSION FRUIT BUTTERCREAM (PAGE 122) AND FRESH PASSION FRUIT PULP. DECORATE WITH A MIX OF ELDERFLOWER BUDS AND SPRIGS.

MASCARPONE BUTTERCREAM (PAGE 112) AND LIGHTLY TOASTED COCONUT CHIPS. THIS IS A SIMPLE FLAVOR PROFILE THAT WORKS WELL.

086

Here's a delectable, rich cake that any chocoholic will simply adore. It's as delicious and comforting as you would expect, and is an excellent all-rounder for any occasion.

chocolate cake

MAKES ONE 8-INCH ROUND CAKE

3½ oz dark chocolate (70% cocoa solids), finely chopped

2–3 tablespoons good-quality instant coffee granules (use decaffeinated if desired)

1 cup boiling water

½ cup hot milk

½ cup (1¾ oz) unsweetened (Dutch) cocoa powder

1 teaspoon vanilla bean paste or natural vanilla extract

1 cup unsalted butter, softened and chopped, plus extra for greasing

1 cup plus 6 tablespoons (10½ oz) raw (demerara) sugar

1 cup (7 oz) dark brown sugar

4 cups (1 lb) self-rising flour or gluten-free self-rising flour

4 eggs, lightly beaten

GREAT FLAVOR COMBINATIONS...

STRAWBERRY BUTTERCREAM (PAGE 119), FRESH WHOLE STRAWBERRIES, AND SMALL PINK AND RED ROSES.

HAZELNUT BUTTERCREAM (PAGE 117) WITH PRALINE SHARDS (PAGE 147). THE STRUCTURAL SHARDS ADD A LITTLE HEIGHT AND DRAMA TO THE CAKE.

CHAI LATTE BUTTERCREAM (PAGE 125) AND LARGE WHITE OR CREAM ROSES. SWEET, SPICY, AND COMFORTING, THIS IS A LOVELY BIRTHDAY CAKE FOR A CHAI LOVER.

Preheat the oven to 325°F. Lightly grease an 8-inch round cake pan.

Place the chocolate and coffee in a heatproof bowl and pour over the boiling water. Stir gently until melted and smooth, and let stand until cool.

Meanwhile, place the hot milk, cocoa powder, and vanilla in a bowl and whisk to combine well, then set aside to cool.

Using an electric mixer, beat the butter and sugars until light and fluffy. With the motor on low speed, add the flour, then the beaten egg, and beat until just combined. Add the chocolate and milk mixtures in alternate batches and beat until well combined. The batter should resemble a coffee-colored frosting.

Spoon the batter into the prepared pan and bake for 35–40 minutes, or until a skewer inserted into the center of the cake comes out clean. Let the cake stand in the pan for 10 minutes, then turn out and transfer to a wire rack to cool completely.

088

In my opinion, nothing says love quite like chocolate does, and this rich, earthy cake is sure to sweeten any relationship. This gluten-free cake is moist and delicious.

flourless chocolate cake

MAKES ONE 8-INCH ROUND CAKE

5½ oz dark chocolate (70% cocoa solids), chopped

1⅓ cup (4¼ oz) unsweetened (Dutch) cocoa powder

1 teaspoon good-quality instant coffee granules (use decaffeinated if desired)

1 teaspoon vanilla bean paste or natural vanilla extract

⅓ cup hot water

⅔ cup (10 tablespoons) unsalted butter, softened, or margarine, plus extra for greasing

1⅓ cups (8½ oz) lightly packed brown sugar

1 cup (3½ oz) almond meal

4 eggs, separated

GREAT FLAVOR COMBINATIONS...
CARDAMOM BUTTERCREAM (PAGE 115) AND CANDIED WALNUTS (PAGE 145).

RICH CHOCOLATE BUTTERCREAM (PAGE 121) WITH PRALINE (PAGE 147) CRUSHED OR IN SHARDS. WHO DOESN'T LIKE PRALINE WITH CHOCOLATE?

Preheat the oven to 350°F. Lightly grease an 8-inch round cake pan and line it with baking parchment.

Place the chocolate in a heatproof bowl over a saucepan of just-simmering water, making sure the base of the bowl doesn't touch the water. Stir occasionally until melted and smooth, then remove from the heat and set aside to cool.

Place the cocoa powder, coffee, vanilla, and hot water in a large bowl and use a whisk to combine well.

Using an electric mixer, beat the butter, sugar, almond meal, melted chocolate, and cocoa mixture until well combined. Add the egg yolks one at a time, beating well after each addition.

Place the egg whites in a clean dry bowl and whisk until soft peaks form. Fold one-third of the egg whites into the chocolate mixture to loosen, then gently fold in the remainder. Pour the mixture into the prepared pan and bake for 60–70 minutes, or until the cake is firm and a skewer inserted into the center comes out clean. Let the cake stand in the pan to cool completely.

carrot cake

There is something so wholesome about carrot cake – yet it's luscious, too. This recipe has been shared and passed along many times over.

MAKES ONE 9-INCH ROUND CAKE

2⅔ cups (10½ oz) all-purpose or gluten-free flour

2 cups (14½ oz) raw (demerara) sugar

¼ cup (1 oz) chopped walnuts

1 teaspoon baking powder

2 teaspoons ground cinnamon

¼ teaspoon freshly grated nutmeg

¼ teaspoon ground cloves

4 eggs, lightly beaten

1 cup vegetable oil, plus extra for greasing

2 teaspoons vanilla bean paste or natural vanilla extract

3 cups (11¼ oz) grated carrot (about 4 medium carrots)

Preheat the oven to 350°F. Lightly grease a 9-inch round cake pan.

Place all the dry ingredients in a large bowl and use a whisk to combine well.

Place the beaten egg, oil, and vanilla in a bowl and use a whisk to combine well. Add the wet mixture to the dry ingredients along with the carrot and stir until well combined.

Pour the batter into the prepared pan and bake for 50–60 minutes, or until a skewer inserted into the center of the cake comes out clean. Let the cake stand in the pan for 10 minutes, then turn out and transfer to a wire rack to cool completely.

GREAT FLAVOR COMBINATIONS...
MASCARPONE BUTTERCREAM (PAGE 112) OR MAPLE BUTTERCREAM (PAGE 113) TOPPED WITH PRALINE (PAGE 147).

HONEY BUTTERCREAM (PAGE 113) AND CHOPPED CRYSTALLIZED GINGER.

MAPLE BUTTERCREAM (PAGE 113) WITH CANDIED WALNUTS (PAGE 145).

090

*I love cardamom. This distinctive, warming spice is
so exotic – some might even say sexy. Pair this cake with
a coffee and you are bound to arouse the senses.*

cardamom cake

MAKES ONE 9-INCH ROUND CAKE

3 cups (12 oz) all-purpose flour

2 teaspoons ground cardamom

1½ teaspoons baking powder

¾ teaspoon baking soda

½ teaspoon salt

4 large eggs, at room temperature

1 teaspoon vanilla bean paste or
natural vanilla extract

1 cup unsalted butter, softened,
plus extra for greasing

2 cups (13 oz) lightly packed
brown sugar

1¼ cups sour cream

**GREAT FLAVOR
COMBINATIONS...**
GINGER BUTTERCREAM
(PAGE 115) AND CHOPPED
CRYSTALLIZED GINGER.

CHAI LATTE BUTTERCREAM
(PAGE 125) WITH CANDIED
WALNUTS (PAGE 145).

HONEY BUTTERCREAM
(PAGE 113) AND A SCATTERING
OF FRESH OR CRYSTALLIZED
VIOLETS (PAGE 157).

Preheat the oven to 350°F. Lightly grease a 9-inch
round cake pan.

Sift the flour, cardamom, baking powder, baking
soda, and salt into a bowl and use a whisk to
combine well.

Place the eggs and vanilla in a bowl and use
a fork to lightly beat them.

Using an electric mixer, beat the butter and sugar
until light and fluffy. With the mixer on medium speed,
gradually add the egg mixture a little at a time,
beating until it is well combined.

Reduce the speed to low, then add the flour mixture
and sour cream in alternate small batches, ending
with the flour mixture.

Spoon the batter into the prepared pan and smooth
the top. Bake for 45–55 minutes, or until a skewer
inserted into the center of the cake comes out dry with
a few moist crumbs attached. Transfer the cake in its
pan to a wire rack to cool completely.

lychee cake

This delightfully light tea cake with a soft crumb is perfect for morning or afternoon tea. I encourage you to try its subtle and unusual flavor.

091

MAKES ONE 8-INCH ROUND CAKE

2 cups plus 2 tablespoons (8½ oz) all-purpose flour

1½ teaspoons baking powder

¼ teaspoon salt

⅔ cup (10 tablespoons) unsalted butter, softened, plus extra for greasing

¾ cup (5¾ oz) superfine sugar

2 eggs, lightly beaten

2 teaspoons vanilla bean paste or natural vanilla extract

1 cup (6½ oz) peeled and seeded fresh lychees (or 20 oz canned lychees, drained), chopped

Preheat the oven to 325°F. Lightly grease an 8-inch cake pan.

Sift the flour, baking powder, and salt into a bowl and use a whisk to combine well.

Using an electric mixer, beat the butter and sugar until light and fluffy. Add the beaten eggs a little at a time, beating well after each addition. Add the vanilla and combine well. With the mixer on low speed, add the flour mixture and beat until just combined. Gently fold in the lychees with a large metal spoon.

Spoon the batter into the prepared pan and bake for 40–45 minutes, or until a skewer inserted into the center of the cake comes out clean. Let the cake stand in the pan for 10 minutes, then turn out and transfer to a wire rack to cool completely.

GREAT FLAVOR COMBINATIONS...
LYCHEE BUTTERCREAM (PAGE 124), FRESH WHOLE AND PEELED LYCHEES, AND HALVED STRAWBERRIES MAKE NATURAL FRIENDS. A FEW SCATTERED STRAWBERRY BLOOMS WILL SET THE CAKE OFF.

MASCARPONE BUTTERCREAM (PAGE 112) AND LARGE ROSE PETALS OF ANY COLOR.

092

One of the best ways to enjoy the cooler months is to make this warming recipe. The sweet and juicy fruit make for a lovely, moist cake. I love anything unusual, and the subtly spiced flavor of this cake is deliciously different.

spiced pear cake

MAKES ONE 8-INCH ROUND CAKE

4 cups (1 lb) all-purpose or gluten-free flour

2 cups (13 oz) lightly packed brown sugar

1½ teaspoons baking soda

1 teaspoon salt

½ teaspoon freshly grated nutmeg

½ teaspoon ground ginger

1 teaspoon ground cinnamon

¼ teaspoon ground cloves

¾ cup (3½ oz) chopped pecans (optional)

2 eggs, lightly beaten

⅔ cup sunflower oil

1 lb peeled, cored, and chopped pear (approximately 8–10 pears)

1 teaspoon vanilla bean paste or natural vanilla extract

Preheat the oven to 325°F. Grease an 8-inch round cake pan.

In a large bowl, mix all the dry ingredients together with a fork until well combined. Set aside.

Put the beaten eggs, oil, pear, and vanilla in a medium bowl and stir to combine.

Pour the wet ingredients into the dry ingredients and use a wooden spoon to mix until well combined.

Pour the batter into the prepared pan and bake for 1 hour, or until a skewer inserted into the center of the cake comes out clean. Let the cake stand in the pan for 10 minutes, then turn out and transfer to a wire rack to cool completely.

GREAT FLAVOR COMBINATIONS... SPICED PEAR CAKE PAIRS WELL WITH CINNAMON, HONEY, VANILLA, MASCARPONE, OR BUTTERSCOTCH BUTTERCREAM. A TOPPING OF HAZELNUT PRALINE (PAGE 147) WOULD ALSO BE DELIGHTFUL.

094

Meringues are quite easy to make – they aren't something you should be intimidated by. They are inexpensive and super-quick for the time-poor, so there is no excuse for not whipping up one of these cakes once in a while.

meringue stack

MAKES TWO MERINGUES

cooking oil spray

4 large egg whites,
at room temperature

1 ¼ cups (9 oz) superfine sugar

½ teaspoon white vinegar

3 teaspoons cornstarch

GREAT FLAVOR COMBINATIONS...
TRY FRESHLY WHIPPED CREAM, FRESH STRAWBERRIES AND RASPBERRIES, AND ROSE PETALS ON TOP AND LAYER WITH WATERMELON AND ROSE JAM (PAGE 148).

LAYER WITH BUTTERSCOTCH BUTTERCREAM (PAGE 114) AND TOP WITH FRESHLY WHIPPED CREAM AND A DRIZZLE OF DARK CHOCOLATE GLAZE (PAGE 128) OR BOOZY SYRUP (PAGE 137).

Preheat the oven to 400°F and set a rack in the middle of the oven. Lightly spray a large baking sheet with cooking oil. Draw two 7-inch circles on a sheet of parchment paper and place it pencil-side down on the baking sheet. (The circles are to use as a guide when spreading the meringue onto the paper.)

Using an electric mixer, beat the egg whites until soft peaks form. With the mixer on medium speed, gradually add the sugar and beat for 1 minute. Increase the speed to high and beat until the whites are thick and glossy and the sugar has dissolved. Reduce the speed to low, add the vinegar, and let the beaters make only a couple of rotations to mix. Fold in the cornstarch.

Using a spatula, scoop the mixture into the circles on the prepared pan and shape into two rounds. Work quickly, as you need to get this into the oven fast. Place the sheet on the middle rack of the oven, immediately reduce the oven temperature to 250°F, and cook for 1 hour 20 minutes. Be careful not to brown the meringue. The crust should be firm, but the meringue will be soft on the inside. Remove from the oven and let cool completely.

crêpe stack

Based on a decadent classic French cake, this is a real treat. Although it looks impressive, it's actually quite easy to make. The flavor of the crêpe stack makes an ideal neutral base to build on.

095

MAKES ONE 8-INCH CRÊPE STACK
(ABOUT 12 CRÊPES)

¼ cup (4 tablespoons) unsalted butter,
plus extra for frying

2½ cups (10½ oz) all-purpose flour

2¾ cups milk

2 large eggs, lightly beaten

GREAT FLAVOR COMBINATIONS...

CHANTILLY CREAM (PAGE 130) WITH POACHED FRUIT (SEE PAGE 154). DUST WITH POWDERED SUGAR.

LAYERS OF CHANTILLY CREAM (PAGE 130) AND FINELY SLICED STRAWBERRIES. TOP WITH AN OPENED LARGE ROSE.

CHANTILLY CREAM (PAGE 130) AND BUTTERSCOTCH BUTTERCREAM (PAGE 114) WITH CRUSHED PRALINE (PAGE 147) OR CANDIED WALNUTS (PAGE 145).

Melt the butter in a small saucepan over low heat, then set aside.

Place the flour, milk, and beaten eggs in a bowl and use a whisk to combine well. Strain through a fine sieve into a pitcher, then stir in the melted butter.

Heat an 8-inch crêpe pan or nonstick frying pan over medium heat. Add a little butter and, when foaming, add ¼–⅓ cup batter, or just enough to cover the bottom of the pan. Immediately tilt the pan to coat the bottom with batter. Cook for 1 minute, or until the crêpe is light golden on the edges, then turn and cook for another 30 seconds. Remove from the pan and repeat with the remaining batter, stacking the crêpes on a plate as you go, with a sheet of baking parchment between each crêpe. Let cool.

Building a cake

I HAVE MADE MY FAIR SHARE

of culinary mistakes over the years — but, then again, who hasn't! As I write this section, I feel that all that experience has paid off and I now know how to build a cake, from splitting and leveling, plating and layering, to stacking and tiering. Some of these techniques can be intimidating at first, but I urge you to have a go, as the results are definitely worth it. There are no high-tech tools required — you'll just need a few bits and pieces from your local cake supplier or kitchenware store. If you are a baker or an experienced home cook, you will have absolutely no trouble mastering these techniques.

098

spliting & leveling

I love to split and level cakes. Whether you split one cake to make two layers, or two cakes to make four, or you bake each layer individually and just need to level them, then these instructions will help. For the record, I even level a single cake to give a lovely, smooth, flat surface to frost and decorate.

There are two different ways to split or level a cake. You can either use a serrated knife or a cake leveler. Personally, I love using a cake leveler, as it makes the process effortless. They are readily available at kitchenware stores and are well worth the investment.

USING A SERRATED KNIFE:

01 Place your cake on a cutting board. Using a ruler, measure out the desired cake level and proceed to cut shallow slits all around the cake at equal intervals.

02 Take a large serrated knife and, holding it at the level you want to cut your cake, cut into the cake horizontally, being guided by the slits you made in the previous step. Work slowly and methodically, moving the knife back and forth in a sawing motion, being careful to keep your knife straight and constantly checking to make sure you are in line with the slits.

03 Using a cake lifter, wide spatula, or flan (tart) pan base, lift away the top of your cake carefully.

01

02

03

02

03

USING A CAKE LEVELER:

01 Follow step 1 opposite, as for the serrated knife method.

02 Take a cake leveler and stand it next to your cake. Position the wires into the slits at the desired height.

03 Cut into the edge of the cake using a gentle sawing motion, gliding the leveler through the cake from one side to the other.

04 Using a cake lifter, wide spatula, or flan (tart) pan base, lift away the top of your cake carefully.

KEEP THINGS LEVEL...

MAKE SURE YOU ALWAYS START WITH A LEVEL WORK SURFACE, AND TRY TO BE AS ACCURATE AS POSSIBLE WHEN CUTTING EACH LAYER. IF THE FIRST TIER IS SLIGHTLY OFF, THEN THE SECOND TIER WILL BE ALSO, AND YOU'LL END UP WITH THE LEANING TOWER OF PISA!

100

There are two types of layered cakes in this book. The first is the basic layered cake with a bare side that reveals each luscious buttercream-filled layer. The second is the layered cake covered with a light whitewash frosting of buttercream (or what some would call a "crumb coat"). In both cases, the bottom tier should be placed on a sturdy cake board or surface that won't bend and will take the total weight of the finished cake.

Basic layered cakes with buttercream centers are simple to put together. Just remember to put slightly less buttercream on the base layer (as the weight of the layers above will cause the base layer to ooze more), and be mindful of crumbs – have a pastry brush, skewer, or tweezers handy to remove them. A pastry brush is also a must to have on hand for brushing away crumbs from your work area.

NOTE: These instructions are for cakes with thin layers, which require no additional support.

BASIC CAKE LAYERING:

01 Smear a little buttercream (2–3 tablespoons) on a cake board to adhere the first cake layer.

02 Using a spatula, smear a generous portion of buttercream on top of the cake and smooth it evenly over the surface. Move the cake gently and take your time to try and prevent raising crumbs on the edges.

03 Use a pastry brush, skewer, or tweezers to remove crumbs as needed.

04 Carefully place a cake layer directly on top of the base layer and push down gently. Add as many subsequent layers as required, then top with a generous layer of buttercream.

01

02

03

04

WHITEWASHED LAYERS:

Follow the instructions for basic cake layering on the opposite page until you have the required number of layers.

01 To whitewash, using a little of the buttercream oozing out of the layers, take a flat-bladed spatula and carefully smear a thin layer of the buttercream gently over the side of the cake.

02 Wipe the spatula clean and dip it in cold water. Holding it upright, move it around the perimeter of the cake in a continuous motion. (The moisture on the spatula will help smooth out the buttercream and give a lovely finish.) A cake turntable can make this process a lot easier.

03 Use a little extra buttercream to fill any gaps, then smooth over again with the damp spatula.

01

02

03

102

stacking cakes

You can stack cakes of equal size, or tiered cakes of gradually reducing size. Stacked cakes, especially tall ones, are best supported and stabilized using doweling rods and cake boards, or pillars and plates. Always consider using these techniques when preparing a cake for a wedding or other important event, even if it's a modest affair and the cake is small. The added support, and the ability to construct and deconstruct the cake, lessens the possibility of heartbreaking accidents and takes the pressure off the person assigned to this job, which may well be you!

I use the simpler doweling rods method for my cakes, where each layer of the cake is placed on its own cake board and the rods are inserted to give extra strength to support the layers on top.

For another level of strength, you could try the pillar and plate technique, using special plastic cake separator/support plates that come with plastic pillars that fit into holes on the bottom of the plates. This is as sturdy a construction as you are ever going to get and a must for any towering sensations.

The tools required for both these techniques are available from specialist cake shops or online. You can also search online for how-to videos of other cake-building techniques.

CAKE BOARDS Cake boards come in rounds, squares, and rectangles, in sizes to match common cake-pan sizes. They are made of either silver foil-coated cardboard, drum (corrugated) cardboard, or Masonite. Use cardboard boards for light cakes, and drum and Masonite (hardboard) boards for multi-tiered and very heavy cakes.

The boards vary in thickness, and range in diameter from 4 to 18 inches. (You could even make your own if you are the handy type.) If you are baking an 8-inch cake, the cake board you require would be the same size or fractionally smaller.

DOWELING RODS Doweling rods are made from either wood or plastic and are used for supporting tiered cakes. Inserted into the lower tiers of a cake, they bear the weight of the tiers above. You could use larger doweling for the larger layers and smaller doweling for the smaller layers. Determining whether you require them is just common sense. The only time when doweling isn't required for a stacked construction is when the lower cakes are very dense and therefore quite stable and able to support lighter cakes, or their own weight, well — a heavy fruit cake would be a good example. However, for light sponges, stabilizing doweling rods are recommended.

It's ideal that a tiered cake be transported as individual layers and assembled on the day of the event at the event venue. The individual layers are easier to pack and transport. You'd be surprised how heavy an assembled tiered cake can get!

Plastic doweling comes in varied sizes. The wider a dowel is in diameter, the greater its stability and support; therefore, with wider dowels fewer are needed. They come solid, or hollow like drinking straws. Consider using thin dowels when the number of servings is important; thin dowels take up less cake space, which equates to more servings.

There is no science to how many doweling rods you should use per tier for each cake, but for an 8-inch cake I would use two thick (½ inch thick) or four thin (¼ inch thick) doweling rods. For larger cakes, use your own discretion. If you are unsure, use more rather than fewer.

I like to use plastic doweling as it's easy to cut – you can just use a heavy-duty pair of kitchen shears, clean pruning shears, or a craft knife. To cut thin wooden doweling, you could probably use kitchen shears, but you might need a small handsaw for thicker pieces.

A central doweling rod can also be placed through all the tiers to stop them from sliding. However, if you opt to do this, make sure you insert it absolutely perpendicular. Push it down into the center of the cake – this may be hard to do through all the layers of cake and cake boards, so you may need to use a doweling rod with a pointed end, and a mallet hammer to carefully force the doweling rod through the cake boards and layers. (This would obviously not work if you were using Masonite cake boards.)

No matter how many doweling rods you use, just make sure that they are evenly spaced so the load is evenly distributed. Remember not to put the rods too close to the edge or outside of where the next tier sits, as the doweling won't be supporting anything.

104

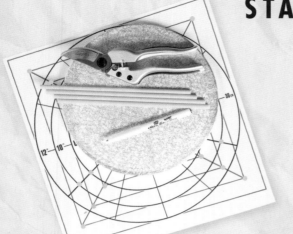

STACKING A CAKE USING DOWELING RODS

way through into the bottom layer of the cake until they touch the base cake board. Using a food-safe pen or knife, mark the spot where each dowel exits the cake (flush with the top of the cake).

04 Remove the pieces of dowel, the cake board, and the plastic template, and cut the doweling rods to the length of the mark, using the shears.

05 Insert the pieces of dowel back into the cake, one by one, using the marked holes as a guide. Gently push the dowels all the way through the cake until they touch the cake board at the bottom. The top of the dowels should be flush with the cake.

06 Place the cake board on top of the dowels again. Now position the smaller, 6-inch cake on the cake board. Decorate the two-tiered cake as desired.

YOU WILL NEED

1 x thick 8½-inch cake board

1 x 6-inch cake board

cake-top marking template (or a skewer)

4 plastic doweling rods (For this two-tiered cake, with the bottom cake being 8 inches and the top cake being 6 inches, I used 4 rods for the bottom layer. For larger cakes, say, 12–16 inches, you might need 6 or 8 pieces of thick dowel.)

food-safe marker pen with edible ink (or a sharp knife)

sturdy kitchen shears or pruning shears

01 Place the bottom 8-inch cake on the larger, thick cake board smeared with 2–3 tablespoons buttercream to adhere. Position a 6-inch cake board on top of the cake.

02 Place a plastic circular template over the cake board (or make four small holes around the outside of the board with a skewer to show the outline).

03 Insert a piece of dowel into each of the four holes that mark out the square, ensuring they are perfectly perpendicular. Push the doweling rods all the

01

02

03

04

05

06

PART
—
02

FILLINGS & FROSTINGS

Butter creams

BUTTERCREAM IS A FILLING OR FROSTING
MADE WITH A BUTTER AND SUGAR BASE.
I do love plain buttercream, made from good-quality
butter and powdered sugar, but I also like to take it
to the next level with the addition of cream cheese
and assorted flavorings. With flavors ranging from
fruit and exotic spices to decadent liqueur and rich
chocolate, these delicious buttercreams are sure to
delight the palate. You'll find the perfect, easy-to-make
cream here for your chosen cake. I've suggested some
flavor pairings, but check out the chart on page 12
for more inspiration. All the recipes in this section
make enough to cover an 8- to 9-inch cake
(or 24 cupcakes).

110

Tips & tricks

**HERE ARE SOME TIPS I HAVE LEARNED ALONG
THE WAY ABOUT MAKING BUTTERCREAMS**

• Always take the time to sift
powdered sugar to prevent lumps.

• You can make buttercream a day ahead and leave it
at room temperature for an easier spreading consistency.

• Buttercream can be refrigerated for several days in an
airtight container, then brought back to room temperature
before using. Whip it briefly to restore its creamy consistency.
(Take care not to overwhip it, as it may curdle.)

• To smooth buttercream on your cake, use a spatula
dipped in water – it makes it so much easier.

• When flavoring buttercream, the general rule is to add
2–3 tablespoons of your desired flavor to the butter. If the
consistency is a little runny, add a little more powdered sugar.

111

vanilla buttercream

A VERSATILE BUTTERCREAM THAT GOES WITH JUST ABOUT EVERY CAKE. IF YOU'RE NOT SURE ABOUT WHAT FILLING OR TOPPING TO USE, THEN VANILLA IS A SURE WINNER. IT IS SUBTLE AND NOT TOO SWEET AND COMPLEMENTS ANY CAKE SERVED WITH FRESH FRUIT. IT ALSO TONES DOWN STRONG FLAVORS LIKE CHOCOLATE AND CARDAMOM.

¾ cup (12 tablespoons) unsalted butter, softened
2¼ cups (9½ oz) powdered sugar, sifted
½ cup (4¼ oz) cream cheese, softened
1 tablespoon plus 1 teaspoon milk
1 teaspoon vanilla bean paste or natural vanilla extract

Using an electric mixer, beat all the ingredients together for 3–5 minutes,
or until light and fluffy. Use it to fill or top the cake of your choice.

mascarpone buttercream

ANOTHER FABULOUS BUTTERCREAM TO EXPERIMENT WITH – IT'S A REAL STANDOUT AND GOES WITH VIRTUALLY ANY CAKE. IT'S SIMPLE, BUT A LITTLE MORE DECADENT THAN PLAIN VANILLA BUTTERCREAM. YOU WILL BE TEMPTED TO EAT THIS FROM THE SPOON, SO BEWARE! IT GOES BEAUTIFULLY WITH ORANGE YOGURT CAKE (PAGE 81) OR LYCHEE CAKE (PAGE 91).

¾ cup (12 tablespoons) unsalted butter, softened
2¼ cups (9½ oz) powdered sugar, sifted
½ cup (4¼ oz) cream cheese, softened
½ cup (4 oz) mascarpone
1 tablespoon plus 1 teaspoon milk
1 teaspoon vanilla bean paste or natural vanilla extract

Using an electric mixer, beat all the ingredients together for 3–5 minutes,
or until light and fluffy. Use it to fill or top the cake of your choice.

maple buttercream

I LOVE MAPLE SYRUP! IT CAN VARY GREATLY IN FLAVOR AND AROMA, FROM A DELICATE BUTTERY POPCORN FLAVOR, THROUGH TO RICH CARAMEL AND COFFEE. TRY THIS WITH VANILLA CAKE (PAGE 82), CHOCOLATE CAKE (PAGE 86), CARROT CAKE (PAGE 89), OR CARDAMOM CAKE (PAGE 90).

¾ cup (12 tablespoons) unsalted butter, softened
2½ cups (11 oz) powdered sugar, sifted
½ cup (4¼ oz) cream cheese, softened
1 tablespoon plus 1 teaspoon milk
1 teaspoon vanilla bean paste or natural vanilla extract
1 generous tablespoon pure maple syrup

Using an electric mixer, beat all the ingredients together for 3–5 minutes, or until light and fluffy. Use it to fill or top the cake of your choice.

113

honey buttercream

HONEY FLAVORS CAN VARY IMMENSELY, AND SOME CHANGE WITH AGE, SO EXPERIMENT AND SEE WHICH TYPE WORKS BEST FOR YOU. PERSONALLY, I JUST LOVE THE FLAVOR OF UNTREATED HONEY. TRY THIS WITH VANILLA CAKE (PAGE 82), ALMOND CAKE (PAGE 84), COCONUT CAKE (PAGE 85), OR CARDAMOM CAKE (PAGE 90).

¾ cup (12 tablespoons) unsalted butter, softened
2¼ cups (9½ oz) powdered sugar, sifted
½ cup (4¼ oz) cream cheese, softened
1 tablespoon plus 1 teaspoon milk
1 teaspoon vanilla bean paste or natural vanilla extract
3–4 tablespoons honey

Using an electric mixer, beat all the ingredients together for 3–5 minutes, or until light and fluffy. Use it to fill or top the cake of your choice.

NOTE: Honey will vary in sweetness, so add it to taste. If you need to add more sweetness, then add a little extra powdered sugar as required.

114

butterscotch buttercream

SQUEALS OF DELIGHT CAME FROM MY KITCHEN WHEN I DISCOVERED THIS RECIPE! BUTTERSCOTCH
IS LIKE CARAMEL'S COUSIN, JUST WITH BUTTERY OVERTONES. TRY THIS SENSATIONAL BUTTERCREAM
WITH VANILLA CAKE (PAGE 82), VICTORIA SPONGE (PAGE 80), ALMOND CAKE (PAGE 84),
COCONUT CAKE (PAGE 85), CHOCOLATE CAKE (PAGE 86), OR CARROT CAKE (PAGE 89).

¾ cup (12 tablespoons) unsalted butter, softened
2¼ cups (9½ oz) powdered sugar, sifted
½ cup (4¼ oz) cream cheese, softened
1 tablespoon plus 1 teaspoon milk
2 teaspoons vanilla bean paste or natural vanilla extract
2 teaspoons butterscotch schnapps

Using an electric mixer, beat all the ingredients together for 3–5 minutes,
or until light and fluffy. Use it to fill or top the cake of your choice.

cinnamon buttercream

THIS IS ONE OF MY FAVORITE BUTTERCREAMS — SWEET, AROMATIC, AND WARMING. IT MAKES
ME THINK OF NIGHTS CURLED UP IN FRONT OF AN OPEN FIRE. IT PAIRS PARTICULARLY WELL WITH
VANILLA CAKE (PAGE 82), CARROT CAKE (PAGE 89), OR CARDAMOM CAKE (PAGE 90).

¾ cup (12 tablespoons) unsalted butter, softened
2¼ cups (9½ oz) powdered sugar, sifted
½ cup (4¼ oz) cream cheese, softened
1 tablespoon plus 1 teaspoon milk
1 teaspoon vanilla bean paste or natural vanilla extract
2 teaspoons ground cinnamon

Using an electric mixer, beat all the ingredients together for 3–5 minutes,
or until light and fluffy. Use it to fill or top the cake of your choice.

ginger buttercream

GINGER IS A SPICE THAT TINGLES ON YOUR TASTE BUDS. TRY THIS BUTTERCREAM WITH
VICTORIA SPONGE (PAGE 80), VANILLA CAKE (PAGE 82), ALMOND CAKE (PAGE 84),
COCONUT CAKE (PAGE 85), CHOCOLATE CAKE (PAGE 86), OR CARROT CAKE (PAGE 89).

¾ cup (12 tablespoons) unsalted butter, softened
2 cups (9 oz) powdered sugar, sifted
1 cup (8½ oz) mascarpone
2–3 tablespoons heavy cream
6 tablespoons (2¼ oz) crystallized ginger, very finely chopped

Using an electric mixer, beat all the ingredients together for 3–5 minutes,
or until light and fluffy. Use it to fill or top the cake of your choice.

115

cardamom buttercream

CARDAMOM IS QUITE EXOTIC AND IS ANOTHER STRONG, AROMATIC, SWEET SPICE THAT
WARMS YOU FROM THE INSIDE. IT ALSO HAS A DELICIOUS, SLIGHTLY CITRUSY CHARACTER AND
MAKES A GORGEOUS BUTTERCREAM FLAVOR. PAIR IT WITH ORANGE YOGURT CAKE (PAGE 81),
VANILLA CAKE (PAGE 82), ALMOND CAKE (PAGE 84), OR CHOCOLATE CAKE (PAGE 86).

¾ cup (12 tablespoons) unsalted butter, softened
2¼ cups (9½ oz) powdered sugar, sifted
½ cup (4¼ oz) cream cheese, softened
1 tablespoon plus 1 teaspoon milk
1 teaspoon vanilla bean paste or natural vanilla extract
2 teaspoons ground cardamom

Using an electric mixer, beat all the ingredients together for 3–5 minutes,
or until light and fluffy. Use it to fill or top the cake of your choice.

hazelnut buttercream

NOT SURPRISINGLY, THIS NUTTY BUTTERCREAM GOES ESPECIALLY WELL WITH
CHOCOLATE CAKE (PAGE 86). ALSO TRY IT WITH VICTORIA SPONGE (PAGE 80),
VANILLA CAKE (PAGE 82), OR ORANGE YOGURT CAKE (PAGE 81).

¾ cup (12 tablespoons) unsalted butter, softened
2¼ cups (9½ oz) powdered sugar, sifted
½ cup (4¼ oz) cream cheese, softened
1 tablespoon plus 1 teaspoon milk
2 teaspoons hazelnut liqueur, such as Frangelico

Using an electric mixer, beat all the ingredients together for 3–5 minutes,
or until light and fluffy. Use it to fill or top the cake of your choice.

117

blackberry and almond buttercream

AAH…YOU JUST HAVE TO TRY THIS. I ABSOLUTELY LOVE THE FLAVOR. BLACKBERRY AND
ALMOND ARE UNEXPECTED FRIENDS, BUT THEY WORK BRILLIANTLY TOGETHER. I LIKE TO USE THIS
WITH VANILLA CAKE (PAGE 82), LEMONADE CAKE (PAGE 83), OR ALMOND CAKE (PAGE 84).

¾ cup (12 tablespoons) unsalted butter, softened
2¼ cups (9½ oz) powdered sugar, sifted
½ cup (4¼ oz) cream cheese, softened
1 tablespoon plus 1 teaspoon milk
½ teaspoon almond extract
1 teaspoon vanilla bean paste or natural vanilla extract
¼ cup blackberry purée (about 1 cup blackberries, puréed and strained)

Using an electric mixer, beat all the ingredients together for 3–5 minutes,
or until light and fluffy. Use it to fill or top the cake of your choice.

118

rose buttercream

THIS BUTTERCREAM CONTAINS ROSEWATER, WHICH SMELLS JUST LIKE FRESH ROSE PETALS.
THE AROMA GETS ME DREAMING ABOUT SUMMERTIME. TRY PAIRING IT WITH
VANILLA CAKE (PAGE 82) OR VICTORIA SPONGE (PAGE 80).

¾ cup (12 tablespoons) unsalted butter, softened
2¼ cups (9½ oz) powdered sugar, sifted
½ cup (4¼ oz) cream cheese, softened
1 tablespoon plus 1 teaspoon milk
1 teaspoon vanilla bean paste or natural vanilla extract
2 teaspoons rosewater
2 drops of natural pink food coloring (optional)

Using an electric mixer, beat all the ingredients together for 3–5 minutes,
or until light and fluffy. Use it to fill or top the cake of your choice.

raspberry and rose buttercream

RASPBERRY AND ROSE MAKE WONDERFUL PARTNERS AND ARE A DELIGHTFUL MATCH WITH A SIMPLE
VICTORIA SPONGE (PAGE 80) OR VANILLA CAKE (PAGE 82), TOPPED WITH FRESH STRAWBERRIES OR
RASPBERRIES. I SEE A SUMMER AFTERNOON TEA ON THE CALENDAR FOR THIS BUTTERCREAM.

¾ cup (12 tablespoons) unsalted butter, softened
2¼ cups (9½ oz) powdered sugar, sifted
½ cup (4¼ oz) cream cheese, softened
1 tablespoon plus 1 teaspoon milk
¼ teaspoon rosewater
¼ cup raspberry purée (about 1 cup raspberries, puréed and strained)
1¾ oz freeze-dried raspberries (available in the snack aisle and online),
pulverized (optional)

Using an electric mixer, beat all the ingredients together for 3–5 minutes,
or until light and fluffy. Use it to fill or top the cake of your choice.

strawberry buttercream

STRAWBERRIES AT THEIR BEST ARE FRAGRANT, JUICY MORSELS OF SWEET LUSCIOUSNESS, AND I DON'T KNOW ANYONE WHO DOESN'T LOVE THEM. THEY MAKE A STUNNING BUTTERCREAM. I LOVE THIS WITH VANILLA CAKE (PAGE 82), LEMONADE CAKE (PAGE 83), OR CHOCOLATE CAKE (PAGE 86).

¾ cup (12 tablespoons) unsalted butter, softened
2¼ cups (9½ oz) powdered sugar, sifted
½ cup (4¼ oz) cream cheese, softened
1 tablespoon plus 1 teaspoon heavy cream
1 teaspoon vanilla bean paste or natural vanilla extract
¼ cup strawberry purée (about 1 cup strawberries, puréed and strained)
1¾ oz freeze-dried strawberries (available in the snack aisle and online), pulverized (optional)

Using an electric mixer, beat all the ingredients together for 3–5 minutes, or until light and fluffy. Use it to fill or top the cake of your choice.

119

blueberry buttercream

HERE'S A WINNER FOR ALL THE BLUEBERRY LOVERS OUT THERE. KIDS WILL LOVE THE GORGEOUS PURPLE COLOR. PAIR IT WITH A VICTORIA SPONGE (PAGE 80) OR VANILLA CAKE (PAGE 82).

¾ cup (12 tablespoons) unsalted butter, softened
2¼ cups (9½ oz) powdered sugar, sifted
½ cup (4¼ oz) cream cheese, softened
1 tablespoon plus 1 teaspoon milk
1 teaspoon vanilla bean paste or natural vanilla extract
¼ cup blueberry purée (about 1 cup blueberries, puréed and strained)
1¾ oz freeze-dried blueberries (available in the snack aisle and online), pulverized (optional)

Using an electric mixer, beat all the ingredients together for 3–5 minutes, or until light and fluffy. Use it to fill or top the cake of your choice.

120

black cherry and vanilla buttercream

LIGHT AND FLUFFY CHERRY BUTTERCREAM WITH A HINT OF VANILLA IS A CREAMY
CLOUD OF DELICIOUSNESS. ENJOY THIS IN SUMMER WITH FRESH, FIRM, AND
FLAVORSOME CHERRIES. PAIR IT WITH VANILLA CAKE (PAGE 82),
ALMOND CAKE (PAGE 84), OR CHOCOLATE CAKE (PAGE 86).

7 tablespoons unsalted butter, softened
2¼ cups (9½ oz) powdered sugar, sifted
¾ cup (7 oz) cream cheese, softened
6 tablespoons (3½ oz) sour cream
1 teaspoon vanilla bean paste or natural vanilla extract
¼ cup black cherry purée (about 8 large cherries, pitted, puréed, and strained)

Using an electric mixer, beat all the ingredients together for 3–5 minutes,
or until light and fluffy. Use it to fill or top the cake of your choice.

●

citrus buttercream

THERE ARE SO MANY OPTIONS HERE, AS YOU CAN USE ANY FRESHLY SQUEEZED AND STRAINED
CITRUS JUICE YOU LIKE. TRY LEMON, ORANGE, BLOOD ORANGE, TANGERINE, LIME, OR MANDARIN.
ONCE YOU'VE CHOSEN THE FLAVOR, CHECK OUT THE FLAVOR-MATCHING CHART, "THIS GOES WITH
THAT" ON PAGE 12, TO SEE WHAT YOU MIGHT PAIR IT WITH. IT WOULD DEFINITELY GO WELL WITH
VANILLA CAKE (PAGE 82), OR TRY ORANGE BUTTERCREAM WITH ORANGE YOGURT CAKE (PAGE 81).

¾ cup (12 tablespoons) unsalted butter, softened
2¼ cups (9½ oz) powdered sugar, sifted
½ cup (4¼ oz) cream cheese, softened
2–3 tablespoons freshly squeezed and strained citrus juice
2 tablespoons finely grated citrus zest

Using an electric mixer, beat all the ingredients together for 3–5 minutes,
or until light and fluffy. Use it to fill or top the cake of your choice.

NOTE: Because some citrus juices are sweeter than others, you may need
to adjust the amount of powdered sugar accordingly.

rich chocolate buttercream

AS THE NAME SUGGESTS, THIS IS VERY RICH, SO BEWARE! IT'S GREAT BETWEEN THE LAYERS
OF A CRÊPE STACK (PAGE 95) THAT HAS BEEN DRENCHED WITH A BOOZY SYRUP (PAGE 137).
IT'S ALSO DELICIOUS USED TO TOP A CAKE THAT'S BEEN FILLED WITH CINNAMON BUTTERCREAM
(PAGE 114), GINGER BUTTERCREAM (PAGE 115), BUTTERSCOTCH BUTTERCREAM (PAGE 114),
STRAWBERRY BUTTERCREAM (PAGE 119), OR VANILLA BUTTERCREAM (PAGE 112).
YOU COULD PAIR THIS WITH VANILLA CAKE (PAGE 82), ORANGE YOGURT CAKE (PAGE 81),
ALMOND CAKE (PAGE 84), OR, OF COURSE, CHOCOLATE CAKE (PAGE 86).

121

¾ cup (12 tablespoons) unsalted butter, softened
2¼ cups (9½ oz) powdered sugar, sifted
½ cup (4¼ oz) cream cheese, softened
½ cup (4¼ oz) mascarpone
1 tablespoon plus 1 teaspoon milk
1 teaspoon vanilla bean paste or natural vanilla extract
2–3 tablespoons unsweetened (Dutch) cocoa powder, or to taste

Using an electric mixer, beat all the ingredients together for 3–5 minutes,
or until light and fluffy. Use it to fill or top the cake of your choice.

passion fruit buttercream

I LOVE THE FLAVOR OF PASSION FRUIT JUST BY ITSELF, SO THIS BUTTERCREAM IS NATURALLY ONE
OF MY FAVORITES. TRY IT WITH VANILLA CAKE (PAGE 82) OR COCONUT CAKE (PAGE 85).

¾ cup (12 tablespoons) unsalted butter, softened
2¼ cups (9½ oz) powdered sugar, sifted
½ cup (4¼ oz) cream cheese, softened
1 tablespoon plus 1 teaspoon milk
1 generous tablespoon passion fruit pulp (you could use the canned variety)

Using an electric mixer, beat all the ingredients together for 3–5 minutes,
or until light and fluffy. Use it to fill or top the cake of your choice.

lemon curd buttercream

THIS BUTTERCREAM HAS A SUBTLE LEMONY FLAVOR AND A LOVELY AROMA WITH JUST A HINT
OF HONEY. PAIR THIS WITH VANILLA CAKE (PAGE 82) OR A CRÊPE STACK (PAGE 95).

¾ cup (12 tablespoons) unsalted butter, softened
2¼ cups (9½ oz) powdered sugar, sifted
½ cup (4¼ oz) cream cheese, softened
¼–⅓ cup Lemon Curd (page 133)

Using an electric mixer, beat all the ingredients together for 3–5 minutes, or until
light and fluffy. Use it to fill or top the cake of your choice.

NOTE: Lemon curd may vary in sweetness, so add it to taste. If it's a little runny,
just add more powdered sugar as needed.

VARIATION: To make a lemon curd cream, whisk 1 cup heavy cream with ½ cup (2 oz)
powdered sugar until firm peaks form, then gently stir in lemon curd to taste.

BUTTERCREAMS

124

elderflower buttercream

A SUBTLE AND DELICATE BUTTERCREAM THAT WOULD BE A TREAT WITH
A VICTORIA SPONGE (PAGE 80) TOPPED WITH FRESH STRAWBERRIES.
IT ALSO GOES BEAUTIFULLY WITH LYCHEE CAKE (PAGE 91).

¾ cup (12 tablespoons) unsalted butter, softened
2¼ cups (9½ oz) powdered sugar, sifted
½ cup (4¼ oz) cream cheese, softened
1 tablespoon plus 1 teaspoon milk
1 teaspoon vanilla bean paste or natural vanilla extract
2–3 tablespoons elderflower cordial (see Note)

Using an electric mixer, beat all the ingredients together for 3–5 minutes,
or until light and fluffy. Use it to fill or top the cake of your choice.

NOTE: Elderflower cordials vary in sweetness, so add it to taste.
If it's a little runny, just add more powdered sugar as needed.

●

lychee buttercream

SWEET AND FLAVORSOME, LOVELY TROPICAL LYCHEES MAKE A DELICIOUS AND UNUSUAL
BUTTERCREAM. THEIR FLAVOR HAS BEEN DESCRIBED AS A CROSS BETWEEN A GRAPE AND A
WATERMELON. YOU JUST HAVE TO TRY THIS WITH LYCHEE CAKE (PAGE 91)! OTHER GOOD PAIRINGS
INCLUDE VICTORIA SPONGE (PAGE 80), VANILLA CAKE (PAGE 82), OR LEMONADE CAKE (PAGE 83).

7 tablespoons unsalted butter, softened
2¼ cups (9½ oz) powdered sugar, sifted
¾ cup (7 oz) cream cheese, softened
6 tablespoons (3½ oz) sour cream
1 teaspoon vanilla bean paste or natural vanilla extract
⅓ cup (2¼ oz) seeded and peeled lychees, finely chopped
(you can use canned lychees, but drain them first)

Using an electric mixer, beat all the ingredients together for 3–5 minutes,
or until light and fluffy. Use it to fill or top the cake of your choice.

chai latte buttercream

THIS BUTTERCREAM IS REALLY SOMETHING SPECIAL AND TASTES JUST
LIKE A CUP OF GOOD CHAI. PAIR IT WITH VANILLA CAKE (PAGE 82),
CHOCOLATE CAKE (PAGE 86), OR CARDAMOM CAKE (PAGE 90).

125

½ cup heavy cream
½ cup milk
1 black tea bag
14 tablespoons unsalted butter, softened
4 cups (1 lb) powdered sugar, sifted
1 cup (8 oz) cream cheese, softened
½ teaspoon ground cinnamon
½ teaspoon ground ginger
¼ teaspoon ground cardamom
¼ teaspoon ground cloves
1 teaspoon vanilla bean paste or natural vanilla extract

Place the cream, milk, and tea bag in a small saucepan over medium heat.
Bring to a simmer, then remove from the heat and set aside to cool.

Using an electric mixer, beat the butter, sugar, cream cheese, spices, and vanilla until combined.

Remove the tea bag from the cream and gradually add the tea-infused cream to the
sugar mixture, beating until well combined. If it's a little runny, just add extra
powdered sugar as needed. Use it to fill or top the cake of your choice.

Glazes, syrups & more

IN THESE PAGES YOU WILL FIND
ALL MANNER OF SWEET DECADENCE.
From fudgy chocolate frosting and glazes
to sumptuous creams, boozy syrups, and luscious
sauces, most of these recipes can be used as fillings
for your naked cakes, but some can also be used
as toppings. You can drizzle the sauces and syrups
over your cakes for extra moistness and to create
a lovely sheen. You'll find all these recipes easy
to make, and they will add another layer of
deliciousness to your baked creation.

128

chocolate fudge frosting

HERE'S A VERY RICH CHOCOLATE FROSTING THAT'S DELICIOUS. USE IT TO TOP A CAKE
FILLED WITH A LIGHTER SWEET CENTER, SUCH AS VANILLA BUTTERCREAM (PAGE 112),
MASCARPONE BUTTERCREAM (PAGE 112), OR CHANTILLY CREAM (PAGE 130).
PAIR THIS WITH ORANGE YOGURT CAKE (PAGE 81) OR CHOCOLATE CAKE (PAGE 86).

MAKES ABOUT 2 CUPS

8 oz dark chocolate (70% cocoa solids), chopped
½ cup (4¼ oz) cream cheese, softened
1 cup (8½ oz) sour cream
1 cup (4½ oz) powdered sugar, sifted

Place the chocolate in a small heatproof bowl over a small saucepan of just-simmering water.
Do not let the base of the bowl touch the water. Heat until melted and smooth,
then remove from the heat and let stand until just cool.

Using an electric mixer, beat together the cream cheese, sour cream, and powdered sugar.
Stir in the cooled chocolate until well combined. Use it to frost the cake of your choice.

●

dark chocolate glaze

THIS IS A WHIPPED FILLING OF CHOCOLATE AND CREAM THAT IS A LITTLE LIGHTER THAN
A GANACHE. IT'S DELICIOUS USED AS A GLAZE OR AS A POURING SAUCE TO TAKE YOUR CAKE
TO ANOTHER LEVEL OF DECADENCE. THIS DARK CHOCOLATE GLAZE WORKS BEAUTIFULLY
WITH CHOCOLATE CAKE (PAGE 86) TOPPED WITH SALTED CARAMEL POPCORN (PAGE 142).
YOU CAN USE MILK CHOCOLATE INSTEAD OF DARK, IF YOU PREFER.

MAKES ABOUT 1 CUP

½ cup light cream or thin whipping cream
8 oz dark chocolate (70% cocoa solids) or milk chocolate, chopped

Place the cream in a small saucepan and bring to a boil over low heat. Remove from the heat,
add the chocolate, and stir until smooth. Use it to top the cake of your choice.

white chocolate glaze

THE BUTTERY, CREAMY FLAVOR OF WHITE CHOCOLATE MAKES THIS GLAZE VERY VERSATILE.
TRY IT WITH VANILLA CAKE (PAGE 82), LEMONADE CAKE (PAGE 83), ALMOND CAKE (PAGE 84),
COCONUT CAKE (PAGE 85), OR LYCHEE CAKE (PAGE 91).

MAKES ABOUT 1⅓ CUPS

½ cup whipping cream
12 oz white chocolate, chopped

Place the cream in a small saucepan and bring to a boil over low heat. Remove from the heat,
add the chocolate, and stir until smooth. Use it to top the cake of your choice.

129

●

limoncello glaze

LIMONCELLO IS AN ITALIAN LIQUEUR MADE FROM FERMENTED LEMONS, WHICH I AM QUITE
PARTIAL TO – ESPECIALLY THE ORGANIC VARIETY! YOU CAN SUBSTITUTE MANDARINELLO, MADE
FROM MANDARINS, OR ARANCELLO, MADE FROM ORANGES. TRY THIS GLAZE WITH COCONUT CAKE
(PAGE 85), WITH HONEY BUTTERCREAM (PAGE 113), AND LEMON CURD (PAGE 133). ALSO PAIR IT
WITH VANILLA CAKE (PAGE 82), LEMONADE CAKE (PAGE 83), OR ALMOND CAKE (PAGE 84).

MAKES ABOUT ½ CUP

1½ cups (6 oz) powdered sugar, sifted
2 teaspoons freshly squeezed and strained lemon juice
2–3 tablespoons limoncello

Whisk all the ingredients together until smooth. Use it to top the cake of your choice.

130

chantilly cream

CHANTILLY CREAM IS A TRADITIONAL FILLING THAT A LOT OF PEOPLE FIND HARD TO PASS UP, ESPECIALLY WHEN ACCOMPANIED WITH STRAWBERRIES. IT GOES WITH EVERYTHING! I LIKE USING IT IN A VICTORIA SPONGE (PAGE 80) OR CHOCOLATE CAKE (PAGE 86) WITH FRESH STRAWBERRIES, IN A MERINGUE STACK (PAGE 94) WITH FRESH FIGS, OR IN A LAYERED CRÊPE STACK (PAGE 95) WITH WATERMELON AND ROSE JAM (PAGE 148) AND BERRIES.

MAKES ABOUT 3⅔ CUPS

2 cups heavy cream
2–3 tablespoons powdered sugar, sifted
1 teaspoon vanilla bean paste or natural vanilla extract

Using an electric mixer, beat the cream, sugar, and vanilla on high speed
until soft peaks form. Use it to fill or top the cake of your choice.

yogurt cream

YOGURT CREAM IS PERFECT FOR THE MORE HEALTH-CONSCIOUS CAKE LOVER. THE CREAM HAS A SLIGHT TARTNESS, WHICH CONTRASTS WELL WITH SWEET FLAVORS. PAIR THIS WITH LEMONADE CAKE (PAGE 83), ALMOND CAKE (PAGE 84), OR CARROT CAKE (PAGE 89).

MAKES ABOUT 1 CUP

1 cup (9¼ oz) plain Greek-style yogurt
3–4 tablespoons pure maple syrup
1 teaspoon vanilla bean paste or natural vanilla extract

Place the yogurt in a cheesecloth-lined sieve over a bowl.
Refrigerate for 2 hours to allow the excess whey to drain.

Place the drained yogurt, maple syrup, and vanilla in a bowl and use a whisk
to combine well. Refrigerate until required. Use it to fill or top the cake of your choice.

dairy-free sweet coconut cream

SUITABLE FOR VEGANS (IF YOU USE MAPLE SYRUP) AND ANYONE WHO LOVES
COCONUT, THIS IS DECADENT AND RICH. IT GOES BEAUTIFULLY WITH
WATERMELON CAKE (PAGE 28) OR CARROT CAKE (PAGE 89).

MAKES ABOUT 1 CUP

2 x 13.5-oz cans full-fat coconut milk (refrigerated for 6 hours or more)
½ teaspoon vanilla bean paste or natural vanilla extract
1 generous tablespoon raw honey or pure maple syrup

Remove the coconut milk from the refrigerator and scoop
the cream off the top, leaving the liquid behind.

Place the coconut cream, vanilla, and honey or maple syrup in a bowl
and use a whisk to combine well. Refrigerate until ready to serve.
Use it to fill or top the cake of your choice.

131

champagne cream

THIS IS PERFECT WITH A SIMPLE VICTORIA SPONGE (PAGE 80) OR VANILLA CAKE
(PAGE 82), BUT YOU CAN ALSO BE ADVENTUROUS WITH THIS ONE. THE TASTE IS SUBTLE
WITH A CITRUS NOTE AND IT BRINGS OUT THE FLAVOR OF FRESH BERRIES.

MAKES ABOUT 2 CUPS

½ cup heavy cream
¼ cup (1¾ oz) cream cheese, softened
2 cups (9 oz) powdered sugar, sifted
¼ teaspoon vanilla bean paste or natural vanilla extract
½ teaspoon finely grated lemon zest
1¼ fl oz (3 tablespoons) Champagne

Using an electric mixer, beat the cream, cream cheese, sugar, vanilla, and lemon zest
until well combined. Gradually add the Champagne and beat until light and fluffy.
Use it to fill or top the cake of your choice.

hot caramel sauce

THIS LUSCIOUS SAUCE COULDN'T BE EASIER TO MAKE. POUR IT OVER VANILLA CAKE (PAGE 82) AND TOP WITH CRUSHED PRALINE (PAGE 147), OR OVER CARDAMOM CAKE (PAGE 90) AND SERVE WITH CHANTILLY CREAM (PAGE 130) AND POACHED PEARS (PAGE 154).

MAKES 1 CUP

1 cup (7 oz) superfine sugar
1½ tablespoons unsalted butter
½ cup whole milk
pinch of sea salt flakes

Place the sugar and ½ cup water in a saucepan over low heat and stir until the sugar has dissolved. Bring to a boil over medium-high heat, then cook, without stirring, until a golden caramel forms, 7–10 minutes.

Remove the pan from the heat and whisk in the butter until melted. Add the milk and stir to combine well. Return the saucepan to the stove, add the salt and stir over medium heat until well combined and slightly thickened, about 2 minutes.

Pour the sauce into a clean, sterilized jar, let cool to room temperature, then store in the refrigerator for up to 2 weeks.

lemon curd

THIS BRINGS BACK SUCH FOND MEMORIES OF TIMES IN THE KITCHEN WITH MY GRANDMOTHER.
TRY IT WITH VICTORIA SPONGE (PAGE 80) AND CHANTILLY CREAM (PAGE 130),
OR VANILLA CAKE (PAGE 82) WITH MASCARPONE BUTTERCREAM (PAGE 112).

MAKES ABOUT 1 ½ CUPS

2 large eggs, lightly beaten
¼ cup (4 tablespoons) unsalted butter
1 cup honey
juice of 2 lemons
finely grated zest of 1 lemon

Place all the ingredients in a heatproof bowl over a saucepan of just-simmering water, making sure the base of the bowl doesn't touch the water. Whisk continuously for 15 minutes, or until the mixture thickens enough to coat the back of a wooden spoon. Remove from the heat, let cool slightly, then pour into a sterilized jar, or let cool and serve on a cake. This will keep in the refrigerator for up to 2 weeks.

133

chocolate mousse

THIS IS BOUND TO BE A FAVORITE AND WOULD BE GREAT ON A MERINGUE STACK (PAGE 94)
DECORATED WITH BALSAMIC CHERRIES (PAGE 152) OR FRESH STRAWBERRIES.

MAKES ABOUT 3 CUPS

6 oz dark chocolate (70% cocoa solids), chopped
½ cup (8 tablespoons) unsalted butter, chopped
3 eggs, separated
1 cup heavy cream
2–3 tablespoons superfine sugar
1 teaspoon vanilla bean paste or natural vanilla extract

Place the chocolate and butter in a heatproof bowl over a small saucepan of just-simmering water, making sure the base of the bowl doesn't touch the water. Stir occasionally until melted and smooth, then remove from the heat and let stand until cool. Using a whisk, add the egg yolks one at a time to the cooled chocolate mixture and combine well.

Place the egg whites in a clean, dry mixing bowl and whisk until soft peaks form.

In another bowl, whisk the cream, sugar, and vanilla just until soft peaks form. Gently fold the cream into the chocolate mixture, then fold in the whisked egg whites. Do not overmix. Use immediately, making sure you don't overwork it as you fill or top your cake.

Syrups

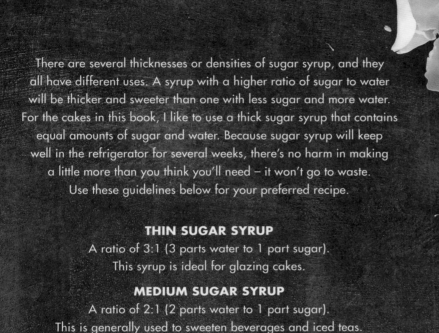

There are several thicknesses or densities of sugar syrup, and they all have different uses. A syrup with a higher ratio of sugar to water will be thicker and sweeter than one with less sugar and more water. For the cakes in this book, I like to use a thick sugar syrup that contains equal amounts of sugar and water. Because sugar syrup will keep well in the refrigerator for several weeks, there's no harm in making a little more than you think you'll need – it won't go to waste. Use these guidelines below for your preferred recipe.

THIN SUGAR SYRUP
A ratio of 3:1 (3 parts water to 1 part sugar).
This syrup is ideal for glazing cakes.

MEDIUM SUGAR SYRUP
A ratio of 2:1 (2 parts water to 1 part sugar).
This is generally used to sweeten beverages and iced teas.

THICK SUGAR SYRUP
A ratio of 1:1 (1 part water to 1 part sugar).
This is used to make candied fruits and sweeten buttercreams or frostings. See the recipe on page 136.

HOW TO GLAZE A CAKE
The traditional way to apply sugar syrup to a cake is to dip a pastry brush in the syrup, then simply brush it on your cake. However, this can get a little messy as cake crumbs can adhere to the brush. I like to use a squeeze bottle (the ones with a cone-shaped top) or a turkey baster to squeeze the syrup very gently onto the cake as evenly as possible.

135

136

basic thick sugar syrup

THIS IS MY BASE RECIPE FOR A THICK SUGAR SYRUP — MY PREFERRED TYPE.

MAKES 1 CUP

¾ cup (5½ oz) superfine sugar
5 fl oz (½ cup plus 2 tablespoons) water

Place the sugar and water in a small saucepan and stir over medium heat until the sugar has dissolved. Bring to a boil, then simmer for 15–20 minutes, or until syrupy. Remove from the heat and let cool. Store the syrup in an airtight container in the refrigerator for up to 2 months.

●

spiced syrup

FEEL FREE TO EXPERIMENT WITH VARIOUS SPICES AND DIFFERENT QUANTITIES OF SPICE. I LOVE TO SOAK MY CARDAMOM CAKE (PAGE 90) WITH THIS SYRUP AND THEN TOP THE CAKE WITH CANDIED ORANGE SLICES (PAGE 149). ALSO TRY IT WITH CARROT CAKE (PAGE 89).

MAKES 1 CUP

1 whole nutmeg
1 cinnamon stick
1 vanilla bean, halved and seeds scraped
1 teaspoon whole black peppercorns
¾ cup (5½ oz) superfine sugar
5 fl oz (½ cup plus 2 tablespoons) water

Place all the ingredients in a saucepan and stir over medium heat until the sugar has dissolved. Bring to a boil, then simmer over medium-low heat for 20 minutes. Remove from the heat, strain, and discard the solids, then let stand until cool. Store the syrup in an airtight container in the refrigerator for up to 2 months.

boozy syrup

BOOZY SYRUPS ADD A GROWN-UP ELEMENT TO A CAKE. MATCH THE ALCOHOL
TO THE FLAVORING OF THE CAKE TO INTENSIFY THE TASTE.

MAKES 1 CUP

¾ cup (5½ oz) superfine sugar
5 fl oz (½ cup plus 2 tablespoons) water
1 fl oz (2 tablespoons) rum or ¼ cup of your favorite liqueur,
such as kirsch or Grand Marnier

Place the sugar, water, and alcohol in a small saucepan and stir over medium heat until the sugar has dissolved. Bring to a boil, then simmer for 15–20 minutes, or until syrupy. Remove from the heat and let cool. Store the syrup in an airtight container in the refrigerator for up to 2 months.

137

orange syrup

FEATURING THE VIBRANT FLAVOR OF JUICY ORANGES, THIS SYRUP WILL FILL THE
HOUSE WITH ITS SWEET AND PLEASING AROMA. YOU'LL FIND THIS RECIPE INCREDIBLY
VERSATILE. IT'S ALSO DELICIOUS POURED OVER PANCAKES OR FRENCH TOAST.

MAKES ABOUT 1½ CUPS

1 cup freshly squeezed and strained orange juice
3 tablespoons freshly squeezed and strained lemon juice
⅓ cup (2½ oz) superfine sugar
⅓ cup orange liqueur, such as Cointreau or Triple Sec

Place all the ingredients in a small saucepan and stir over low heat until the sugar has dissolved. Simmer for 4 minutes, or until a light syrup forms. Remove from the heat and let cool or serve warm. Store the syrup in an airtight container in the refrigerator for up to 2 months.

PART
03

THE FINISHING TOUCHES

Sweet finishes

OK, YOU'VE PUT THE ICING ON THE CAKE...
now it's time to think about adding a few sweet
adornments for some wow factor. In this chapter you
will find innovative ideas for little jewels of flavor,
which will add another layer of deliciousness and
flair to your creation. Many of the recipes are
ridiculously easy to make, yet they all look so
impressive that your guests will be swooning.
Enjoy exploring these pages and making
some sweet memories.

142

salted caramel popcorn

CARAMEL POPCORN HAS A NOSTALGIC APPEAL FOR ME AS IT WAS CONSIDERED A REAL TREAT WHEN I WAS YOUNG. WITH SOME ADDED SALT, THIS IS EVEN MORE TEMPTING — AND IT'S JUST SO EASY TO MAKE. IF YOU WANT TO SAVE TIME, USE READY-POPPED CORN AND JUMP STRAIGHT TO THE CARAMEL PART OF THE RECIPE. THIS RECIPE MAKES ABOUT 4 CUPS, SO YOU'LL HAVE EXTRA TO NIBBLE ON.

MAKES ABOUT 4 CUPS

2–3 tablespoons vegetable oil
⅓ cup dried popcorn kernels
½ cup (3¾ oz) sugar
¼ cup (4 tablespoons) unsalted butter, chopped
2 teaspoons sea salt flakes

Place the oil in a large saucepan with a lid over medium heat. To test if the oil is hot enough, add a couple of popcorn kernels to the pan — they should spin around in a circle. Add the remaining kernels, cover, and cook until the corn starts to pop. Shake the pan gently until the corn stops popping, about 7 minutes, then remove from the heat. Spread the popcorn over a parchment paper–lined baking sheet and discard any unpopped kernels in the bottom of the pan.

Place the sugar in a small saucepan over medium heat and cook, shaking the pan regularly, until the sugar has dissolved. Reduce the heat to low and cook until the caramel is a deep amber color, tilting the pan gently to make sure the color is even. Carefully add the butter and stir for 5 minutes, or until well combined. Increase the heat, bring to a boil, then reduce the heat again and simmer, without stirring, for another 5–7 minutes, or until thick and caramelized.

Remove the pan from the heat and stir in the salt. Carefully pour the hot caramel over the popcorn on the lined baking sheet. Set aside to cool, then break it into pieces.

NOTE: You may like to make some caramel sauce to pour over the top of your salted caramel popcorn. See the Hot Caramel Sauce recipe (page 132).

PAIR IT WITH...
VANILLA CAKE (PAGE 82) AND HOT CARAMEL SAUCE
(PAGE 132), OR A CRÊPE STACK (PAGE 95) WITH
CHANTILLY CREAM (PAGE 130) AND HOT CARAMEL SAUCE.

144

apple compote

APPLE COMPOTE IS A NICE ADDITION TO NAKED CAKES FOR A MORNING OR AFTERNOON TEA
GATHERING WITH FAMILY AND FRIENDS, ESPECIALLY IN THE COOLER MONTHS OF THE YEAR.
SERVE ON TOP OF A CAKE AS A DECORATION, OR ON THE SIDE.

MAKES ABOUT 2 CUPS

5 green apples, peeled, cored and cut into chunks
1 cup water
¼ teaspoon ground cinnamon
¼ teaspoon ground ginger
2 cloves
1 teaspoon vanilla bean paste or natural vanilla extract
zest and juice of ½ lemon
¼ cup (1¾ oz) raw (demerara) sugar

Combine all the ingredients in a saucepan over medium heat and slowly bring to a simmer.
Cover and cook for 10 minutes, or until the apples are soft but still firm and holding their shape.
Don't cook them too long, or they will turn to mush!

Remove from the heat, then discard the cloves and leave the compote to stand until cool.
Store in an airtight container in the refrigerator for up to 1 week.

PAIR IT WITH...
ANY TYPE OF SPICED CAKE, SUCH AS CARDAMOM CAKE
(PAGE 90) WITH A CREAMY VANILLA BUTTERCREAM (PAGE 112).
IT'S ESPECIALLY NICE ON THE CRÊPE STACK (PAGE 95).

candied walnuts

CANDIED WALNUTS ARE JUST SO DELICIOUS — I EVEN LOVE THEM IN A SALAD!
HOWEVER, THEY LOOK PARTICULARLY BEAUTIFUL PILED ON TOP OF A CAKE.

145

MAKES ABOUT 2 CUPS

2 cups (8 oz) shelled walnuts
⅓ cup pure maple syrup
pinch of sea salt flakes

Place the walnuts, maple syrup, and salt in a large frying pan over medium heat. Cook, stirring regularly, for 3–5 minutes, or until the nuts start to caramelize. Remove from the heat and let cool before serving. Store in an airtight container at room temperature for a couple of days.

PAIR THEM WITH...
CARROT CAKE (PAGE 89) AND HONEY
BUTTERCREAM (PAGE 113), OR CHOCOLATE CAKE
(PAGE 86) WITH MAPLE BUTTERCREAM (PAGE 113).
THEY ARE ALSO LOVELY SCATTERED ON TOP OF
APPLE COMPOTE (SEE OPPOSITE).

praline

MAKES ONE 6 X 4-INCH SHEET

½ cup (3¾ oz) superfine sugar
2 teaspoons malt vinegar
¾ cup (4¼ oz) unsalted nuts of choice, toasted

147

Line a baking sheet with parchment paper. Place the sugar, ⅓ cup water, and the vinegar in a small saucepan over low heat and stir until the sugar has dissolved. Increase the heat to medium and bring to a boil, then reduce the heat to low and simmer without stirring for 10 minutes, or until the caramel reaches 280–309°F, or hard-crack stage, on a candy thermometer.

At this point, you need to give the caramel your full attention. The longer you cook it, the darker it will become and it can quickly go from perfect to burnt. If you don't have a candy thermometer, drop a little syrup into a cup of cold water. If the toffee sets immediately and you can crack it between your fingers, then it's ready. Stir in the nuts, then pour the mixture onto the lined pan.

Let stand for 15 minutes, or until hard and brittle. Break into whatever size pieces you like, or blitz in a food processor until coarsely or finely chopped. Store in an airtight container at room temperature for up to 1 week or in the freezer for up to 1 month.

PAIR IT WITH...
TRY AN ALMOND PRALINE WITH CHOCOLATE CAKE (PAGE 86) AND
RICH CHOCOLATE BUTTERCREAM (PAGE 121), OR A HAZELNUT
PRALINE WITH CHOCOLATE CAKE AND HAZELNUT BUTTERCREAM
(PAGE 117) OR MASCARPONE BUTTERCREAM (PAGE 112).

watermelon and rose jam

I DON'T KNOW A SOUL WHO DOESN'T DELIGHT IN THE OLD-SCHOOL CHARM OF THIS JAM, OR WHO HASN'T BEEN HYPNOTIZED BY ITS AROMA. BOTTLE IT UP FOR GIFTS THAT WILL DELIGHT.

MAKES ABOUT 2 CUPS

1 ¼ lb ripe watermelon flesh, chopped
2 cups (14 oz) superfine sugar
juice of 1 lemon
small handful organic rose petals or rosewater to taste

Place the watermelon in a bowl and sprinkle it with the sugar and lemon juice. Cover and let stand for at least 4 hours, or overnight if possible.

Transfer the watermelon mixture to a heavy-bottomed saucepan and bring to a boil over medium heat. Reduce the heat to low and simmer, stirring regularly, for 1 hour.

Using a handheld blender, process the mixture until it's as smooth or chunky as you desire. When ready, the jam will be quite thin, but should resist sliding down a plate if you hold it upright. Stir in the petals or rosewater and pour the hot jam into sterilized jars. Refrigerate for up to 2 weeks.

PAIR IT WITH...
VANILLA CAKE (PAGE 82) AND CHANTILLY CREAM (PAGE 130).
IT'S ALSO GREAT IN A CRÊPE STACK (PAGE 95)
WITH CHANTILLY CREAM AND BERRIES.

candied orange slices

MAKE THESE ONCE AND YOU'LL MAKE THEM AGAIN AND AGAIN. YOU DON'T NEED TO STOP
AT ORANGES, AS LEMONS, BLOOD ORANGES, AND GRAPEFRUIT ALL WORK WELL TOO.
TRY DIPPING THEM IN MELTED CHOCOLATE FOR A REAL FLAVOR SENSATION.

149

MAKES ABOUT 12 SLICES

½ cup (3¾ oz) superfine sugar
2 oranges, cut into ¼-inch-thick slices, ends and seeds discarded

Place the sugar and 1½ cups water in a saucepan and stir over medium heat until the sugar
has dissolved. Bring to a boil, then add the orange slices and simmer for 20 minutes,
or until the liquid has reduced to a thin syrup and the orange slices are translucent.

Reduce the heat to low and simmer until the syrup is thick and the slices
are tender but still intact, about 10 minutes.

Drain through a sieve placed over a bowl, then transfer the orange slices to a wire rack to cool.

Reserve the syrup for another use, or drizzle the cooled syrup on top
of a warm cake and add the orange slices to garnish. The candied orange slices
(pictured on page 38) can be refrigerated for up to 2 weeks.

PAIR THEM WITH...
ORANGE YOGURT CAKE (PAGE 81) WITH CHANTILLY
CREAM (PAGE 130) AND VANILLA BUTTERCREAM (PAGE 112)
OR MASCARPONE BUTTERCREAM (PAGE 112). THEY ALSO
WORK REALLY WELL ON CARDAMOM CAKE (PAGE 90) SOAKED
WITH A SPICED SYRUP (PAGE 136).

segmented oranges

SEGMENTED ORANGES ARE PLEASING, FRESH, AND FLAVORSOME AND ADD A JUICY BURST OF GOODNESS TO YOUR CAKES. I LOVE THE JEWELED LOOK OF THE CLEAN-CUT SEGMENTS. YOU CAN USE THIS TECHNIQUE FOR OTHER CITRUS FRUIT, LIKE GRAPEFRUIT AND LEMONS, TOO.

Using a sharp paring knife and downward, even strokes, peel away the skin and pith of the fruit. Take your time to remove it all carefully. (Leaving any pith on will result in a bitter flavor.) Be careful not to take away too much of the fruit, and try to keep the natural shape.

Cut between the membranes of the orange, as shown opposite, trying to keep as much flesh in each segment as possible. Continue until you have cut each segment away.

If you like, cut the oranges over a plate or bowl to catch the juice, which is delicious mixed with a little orange blossom water and sugar.

PAIR THEM WITH...
SEGMENTED ORANGES ARE GREAT AS A FRESH TOPPING ON AN ORANGE YOGURT CAKE (PAGE 81), CARDAMOM CAKE (PAGE 90), ALMOND CAKE (PAGE 84), OR CHOCOLATE CAKE (PAGE 86). JUST ADD A LITTLE CHANTILLY CREAM (PAGE 130).

152

balsamic cherries

I HAVE A THING FOR BALSAMIC CHERRIES, ESPECIALLY WHEN TEAMED WITH RICH, DARK CHOCOLATE. FOR LARGE CHRISTMAS PARTIES, I OFTEN MAKE SEVERAL PAVLOVAS WITH CHOCOLATE GANACHE AND TOP THEM WITH THESE CHERRIES.

MAKES ABOUT 2 CUPS

1 ½ lb fresh black cherries, pitted
¾ cup (5½ oz) superfine sugar
⅓ cup balsamic vinegar

Place all the ingredients in a large saucepan and stir over high heat for 4–5 minutes, or until the sugar has dissolved. Using a slotted spoon, remove the cherries from the pan and place in a bowl.

Reduce the heat and simmer the syrup in the pan for 4–5 minutes, or until reduced by half. Pour the syrup over the cherries and refrigerate until serving, or store in sterilized jars in the refrigerator for up to 2 weeks.

PAIR THEM WITH...
THESE CHERRIES MAKE A BEAUTIFUL DECORATION FOR ALMOND CAKE (PAGE 84), ORANGE YOGURT CAKE (PAGE 81), OR LEMONADE CAKE (PAGE 83). PAIR THEM WITH VANILLA CAKE (PAGE 82) AND HONEY BUTTERCREAM (PAGE 113), OR A CRÊPE STACK (PAGE 95) WITH CHANTILLY CREAM (PAGE 130) AND A MIXTURE OF COLORFUL PANSIES OR VIOLAS.

caramelized figs

I JUST LOVE CARAMELIZED FIGS. TEAMED WITH A LUSCIOUS BUTTERCREAM, THEY MAKE A STUNNING TREAT. I LOVE THEM WITH A MERINGUE STACK (PAGE 94) AND CHANTILLY CREAM (PAGE 130).

153

SERVES 4

4 figs, halved
2–3 tablespoons brown sugar
juice of 1 lemon
pure maple syrup to drizzle (optional)

Preheat the oven to 325°F.

Place the figs cut-side up in a baking dish. Sprinkle with the sugar
and pour the lemon juice evenly over the top.

Bake for 20–25 minutes, or until the sugar starts to caramelize.
Remove from the oven and let cool.

Place the caramelized figs in the center of your cake and drizzle with maple syrup, if desired.
You can store the figs in an airtight container before serving, but they're best served fresh.

PAIR THEM WITH...
CHOCOLATE CAKE (PAGE 86) WITH RICH CHOCOLATE
BUTTERCREAM (PAGE 121), OR LEMONADE CAKE (PAGE 83)
OR VANILLA CAKE (PAGE 82) WITH MASCARPONE BUTTERCREAM
(PAGE 112). PILE THEM ON TOP OF ORANGE YOGURT CAKE
(PAGE 81) WITH CHANTILLY CREAM (PAGE 130) ON THE SIDE.
THESE ARE ALSO BEAUTIFUL USED TO DECORATE A LARGE
WHEEL OF BRIE CHEESE.

154

Poached fruits make a lovely decoration or accompaniment for a naked cake, just as long as they aren't too soft. They are the perfect addition to an afternoon tea cake or simple sponge.

poached fruit

POACHED PEARS

A GREAT POACHED PEAR IS DETERMINED BY THE RIPENESS OF THE FRUIT. CHOOSE PEARS THAT AREN'T TOO HARD OR TOO RIPE EITHER. OVERRIPE FRUIT WILL TURN TO MUSH, AND UNDERRIPE FRUIT WILL BE HARD, TASTE TERRIBLE, AND DISCOLOR. CHOOSE A HEAVY-BOTTOMED SAUCEPAN THAT WILL HOLD THE PEARS SNUGLY WITHOUT SQUASHING THEM. TRY THREE HALVES ON TOP OF YOUR CAKE AND THE REST SERVED ON THE SIDE. A SMALL SINGLE PEAR ALSO LOOKS GREAT AS A CENTERPIECE ON A LARGE CAKE.

MAKES 6

2½ cups (18 oz) superfine sugar

1 quart filtered water

6 pears (Bosc are my favorite)

Place the sugar and water in a heavy-bottomed saucepan just large enough to fit the pears in a single layer. Stir over low heat until the sugar has dissolved, then increase the heat to medium and bring to a simmer.

Meanwhile, to prepare the pears, use a melon scoop to remove the core of the pear, working from the base. Using a vegetable peeler and starting from the top and moving downwards, peel the pears and place them in the pan right-side up. Cover with a cartouche (see Note), then the lid and cook for 10–15 minutes, or until the fruit can easily be pierced with a knife. Remove from the heat and let cool with the cartouche still on top. Refrigerate until needed.

NOTE: A cartouche is a round piece of parchment or waxed paper that is placed directly on the surface of whatever you are cooking to help reduce evaporation. You will need to make your cartouche before you start cooking.

TO MAKE A CARTOUCHE: Tear off a piece of parchment paper that is slightly bigger than you need. Turn the pan you're going to be cooking with upside down on the paper. Draw around the pan with a pencil and then cut the circle out with kitchen scissors, removing all traces of pencil. Fold the circle in half, then in half again and then half again. Now snip the triangular tip off the paper with kitchen scissors to make a small hole, and unfold the paper. You should have a round of paper that is the exact circumference of your pan.

PAIR THEM WITH...
SPICED PEAR CAKE
(PAGE 92) AND HONEY
BUTTERCREAM (PAGE 113) OR
BUTTERSCOTCH BUTTERCREAM
(PAGE 114), A SCATTERING
OF ROASTED HAZELNUTS,
AND SOME CHANTILLY CREAM
(PAGE 130) ON THE SIDE.

POACHED STONE FRUITS

FOR STONE FRUIT, YOU NEED TO CHOOSE PERFECTLY RIPE FRUIT; OTHERWISE THEIR SKINS WON'T SLIP OFF IN THE BLANCHING PROCESS. HOWEVER, THEY CAN'T BE TOO RIPE, OR THEY WILL TURN TO MUSH DURING POACHING. FOR POACHED STONE FRUIT I FIND YOU ONLY REQUIRE HALF THE AMOUNT OF SUGAR NEEDED FOR PEARS, AS THEY ARE SO INTRINSICALLY SWEET. CHOOSE A HEAVY-BOTTOMED SAUCEPAN THAT WILL HOLD THE FRUIT SNUGLY WITHOUT SQUASHING THEM.

MAKES 4-5

4–5 stone fruits, such as apricots, peaches, plums, or nectarines (depending on the size)

iced water

1¼ cups (9 oz) superfine sugar

1 quart filtered water

Peaches and nectarines will need their skins removed before poaching. To do this, bring a medium saucepan of water to a rapid boil. Have a bowl of iced water ready to drop the fruit into after blanching. Using a slotted spoon, plunge the fruit into the boiling water for about 20 seconds, then remove with the spoon and plunge straight into the iced water. You should now be able to easily remove the skins.

Cut the fruit in half following the natural line around the middle. Carefully twist to separate the halves without bruising the flesh, then remove the pit.

Place the sugar and water in a large heavy-bottomed saucepan over low heat and stir until the sugar has dissolved. Bring to a simmer, then add the fruit, making sure the fruit is fully submerged. Cover with a cartouche (see opposite), then put on the lid and increase the heat to medium. Simmer for 10–15 minutes, or until the fruit can easily be pierced with a knife.

Remove from the heat and let stand with the cartouche still on top until cool. Refrigerate until needed.

PAIR THEM WITH...

TRY POACHED APRICOTS WITH VANILLA CAKE (PAGE 82) AND HONEY BUTTERCREAM (PAGE 113) OR MASCARPONE BUTTERCREAM (PAGE 112), OR POACHED PLUMS WITH CHOCOLATE CAKE (PAGE 86), CINNAMON BUTTERCREAM (PAGE 114), AND SOME SHAVINGS OF DARK CHOCOLATE ON TOP. POACHED NECTARINES GO WELL WITH A VICTORIA SPONGE (PAGE 80) WITH CHANTILLY CREAM (PAGE 130) AND MAPLE BUTTERCREAM (PAGE 113).

156

crystallized flowers

THERE ARE MANY BLOOMS THAT LEND THEMSELVES TO CRYSTALLIZATION — PANSIES, ROSES, AND VIOLETS ARE JUST A FEW, BUT HERE I HAVE CHOSEN VIOLAS. A SMALL LAYERED CAKE TOPPED SOLELY WITH MASSES OF CRYSTALLIZED BLOOMS CAN LOOK DIVINE.

edible organic violas
superfine sugar (the amount needed will vary depending
on the amount of flowers you have – start with about ½ cup/3½ oz)
1 egg white

Pick the flowers when the dew is dry and select those that are blemish-free.

Line two baking sheets with parchment paper. Place the sugar on a large dinner plate or another baking sheet.

Whisk the egg white with a fork until bubbly but not frothy. With a small brush, gently and lightly paint the egg white onto all parts of the flower. I like to start with the underside.

Sprinkle the flowers with sugar to cover well. Shake off any surplus sugar, then place the flowers right-side up on the prepared pans to dry in a warm room. This should take 12–36 hours. When ready, the flowers should be brittle. To hasten drying you could use a dehydrator or place the flowers in a 150°F oven, with the door open, for a few hours.

When thoroughly dried, place the flowers in an airtight container between layers of parchment paper and store in a cool, dry place. They will keep for about a week.

HANDCRAFTED SUGAR PASTE FLOWERS
YOU COULD ALSO USE SUGAR PASTE FLOWERS INSTEAD. THERE IS AN ART TO MAKING THESE, WHICH WOULD FILL THE PAGES OF ANOTHER BOOK. THEREFORE, IF YOU ARE TIME-POOR (LIKE ME), IT'S EASIER TO SOURCE THESE BEAUTIES FROM YOUR LOCAL BAKERY, CAKE SUPPLY STORE, OR EVEN ONLINE.

157

Flowers & leaves

FLOWERS AND LEAVES HAVE BEEN USED IN COOKING FOR CENTURIES, both for flavor and as decoration. I delight in using them on almost all my cakes (see the following pages for a selection of my favorites). They are a fun way of adding color and interest, while also showing off your artistic skills. Many flowers and leaves are edible, but before you put them anywhere near your edible creations, ensure that they are nonpoisonous and pesticide-free. Proper identification is absolutely essential, so be certain that you know what species you are using. If in doubt, it's safer not to use it.

160

Take care! I have seen poisonous blooms used on cakes before, so always do your research before you use any plant. If in doubt, don't use it.

GROWING EDIBLE FLOWERS A simple window box or balcony is all you need to create an edible Eden of flowering cake decorations. Growing your own edible flowers can definitely enhance your culinary repertoire. There is a world of flower-eating possibilities out there! Maybe start with some herb flowers like basil, borage, lavender, mint, or rosemary. For edible blooms, nasturtiums are one of the easiest to grow – I love their trailing and cheery nature. Pansies and violas are beautiful and not too challenging either.

For optimal beauty and flavor, you should choose blooms at their peak. Select perky, colorful flowers without any discolorations or imperfections. Ideally, harvest flowers early in the morning or late afternoon or evening – especially in summer. The heat of the day can cause flowers to droop and wilt readily. Once they are picked, take good care of the flowers to preserve them well.

Edible flowers are delicate and perish quickly after harvesting. Store them in a container with a layer of damp paper towel underneath and on top.

DECORATING A CAKE WITH FRESH FLOWERS Fresh flowers for decorating should be added to cakes only just before serving, if possible. If you need them to last a long time, maybe practice with your chosen blooms before a special event, to see how long they will last. There are a couple of ways I would crown, or top, a cake with flowers, but for the tiered cakes in this book, you would use the following technique:

1 Gather your chosen flowers. Cut the stems on a 45-degree angle with garden shears and place them in water for a good drink.

2 When you are ready, trim the flower stems so they will sit neatly and flat on the top of your cake, or in your desired position.

**FLOWER & FRUIT
FLAVOR PAIRINGS**

IF YOU WOULD LIKE TO
MATCH YOUR EDIBLE
FLOWERS WITH FRUIT
DECORATIONS, THEN HERE
IS A GUIDE TO SOME
PAIRINGS THAT WORK
PARTICULARLY WELL.

**ELDERFLOWERS
WORK WELL WITH:**
APPLE, CHERRY,
GOOSEBERRY, GRAPE (GREEN),
HONEYDEW MELON,
NECTARINE, PEACH,
RASPBERRY, STRAWBERRY

**HIBISCUS PETALS
WORK WELL WITH:**
BANANA, CRANBERRY,
PINEAPPLE, RED CURRANT

**JASMINE FLOWERS
WORK WELL WITH:**
GUAVA, LYCHEE, MANGO,
PINEAPPLE, STRAWBERRY

**LAVENDER FLOWERS
WORK WELL WITH:**
BLUEBERRY, LEMON,
ORANGE, PEAR,
ROSEMARY, STRAWBERRY

**ROSE PETALS
WORK WELL WITH:**
APPLE, BERRIES, CHERRY,
CUSTARD APPLE, FIG,
GUAVA, LYCHEE, MELON,
STONE FRUITS

**VIOLET PETALS
WORK WELL WITH:**
BLACK CURRANT, FIG, GRAPE
(BLACK), HONEYDEW MELON

161

Wrap the stems with floral tape so the sap from the plant doesn't make contact with the cake.

Position the flowers on the cake as you choose.

If you want to place blooms on tiers and you are concerned that the blooms will move or fall, push a little floral wire into the stem of the flower, then wrap the stem in floral tape and insert the flower stem into the cake where you like.

A NOTE ABOUT SAFETY When using any flowers with cakes and food, it's vital to source organic blooms that have not been sprayed with chemicals. If using non-organic blooms, ensure they do not make direct contact with any edible part of your cake. Always wrap the stems thoroughly in floral tape and remove the stamens if advised. Arm yourself with a reputable online plant guide like Cornell University's (gardening.cornell.edu/homegardening). Books recommended for reading about edible flowers include *The Edible Flower Garden*, by Rosalind Creasy; *Cooking with Edible Flowers*, by Miriam Jacobs; *The Scented Kitchen: Cooking with Flowers*, by Frances Bissell; *Good Enough to Eat*, by Jekka McVicar; and *Edible Flowers: From Garden to Palate*, by Cathy Wilkinson Barash.

162

ALLIUM
Allium spp.

ALL BLOSSOMS FROM THE *ALLIUM* GENUS (ONIONS, CHIVES, GARLIC, GARLIC CHIVES, AND LEEKS) ARE EDIBLE, AND THERE ARE MORE THAN 500 SPECIES. LIKE FIREWORKS FROZEN IN MID-EXPLOSION, THESE BLOOMS ARE DELIGHTFUL, AND I JUST LOVE THE POM-POM HEADS OF THE MORE ORNAMENTAL TYPES. THE COLORS CAN BE ANYTHING FROM PURPLE, LILAC, ROSE PINK, AND CRIMSON RED TO POWDER BLUE, LEMON YELLOW, AND PURE WHITE. THE SIZES ALSO VARY GREATLY.

BASIL

Ocimum basilicum

YOU WILL FIND BASIL'S TINY DAISY-LIKE
BLOSSOMS CLUSTERED ON A SINGLE
SPIKE AT THE TOP OF THE PLANT. THEY
COME IN A VARIETY OF COLORS, FROM
WHITE TO PINK AND LAVENDER. THE
FLAVOR OF THE BLOOMS IS SIMILAR TO
THAT OF THE LEAVES, BUT MILDER. THEY
MAKE A NICE DECORATIVE GARNISH FOR
A CHEESE WHEEL CAKE (SEE PAGE 60).

BORAGE

Borago officinalis

THE CAREFREE AZURE FLOWERS OF BORAGE HAVE A STAR-SHAPED,
BLACK CENTER AND A CLEAR WHITE EYE. BOTH THE LEAVES AND
FLOWERS OF BORAGE HAVE A FAINT CUCUMBER FLAVOR.
WARNING: PREGNANT OR LACTATING WOMEN SHOULD AVOID BORAGE.

166

CARNATION

Dianthus caryophyllus

THESE BLOSSOMS HAVE A FLAVOR SIMILAR TO THEIR SWEET AROMA — SPICY,
FLORAL AND CLOVELIKE. USE ONLY THE PETALS AND REMOVE THE BITTER WHITE
HEEL AT THE BASE OF THE PETAL. THE COLORS RANGE FROM WHITE AND YELLOW
THROUGH TO PINK AND RED, BUT OTHER COLORS ARE ALSO AVAILABLE.

CHIVE
Allium schoenoprasum

A MEMBER OF THE ONION FAMILY, CHIVES
HAVE DELICATE, STAR-SHAPED FLOWERS
WITH SIX PETALS. THEY ARE A BEAUTIFUL
PINKISH LILAC COLOR AND LOOK GORGEOUS
AS A DECORATION ON NAKED CAKES.

168

CHRYSANTHEMUM
Glebionis coronaria

THESE BLOOMS COME IN A RANGE OF COLORS, FROM RED
AND WHITE TO YELLOW, AND ALSO VARY IN FLAVOR FROM
SLIGHTLY BITTER TO SPICY. USE ONLY THE PETALS.

CITRUS BLOSSOM

Orange *(Citrus × sinensis)*, lemon *(Citrus limon)*,
lime *(Citrus aurantifolia)*, grapefruit *(Citrus × paradisi)*,
kumquat *(Citrus japonica)*

CITRUS BLOOMS ARE GENERALLY WHITE, OVERWHELMING IN SCENT, AND PRONOUNCED IN FLAVOR,
SO USE THEM SPARINGLY AS AN EDIBLE GARNISH. THEY ARE IDEAL FOR CRYSTALLIZING.

FLOWERS & LEAVES

170

CORNFLOWER

Centaurea cyanus

A STRIKING AND ATTRACTIVE EDIBLE BLOOM
WITH BRIGHT, CELEBRATORY BLUE FLOWERS,
ALSO KNOWN AS BACHELOR'S BUTTON.

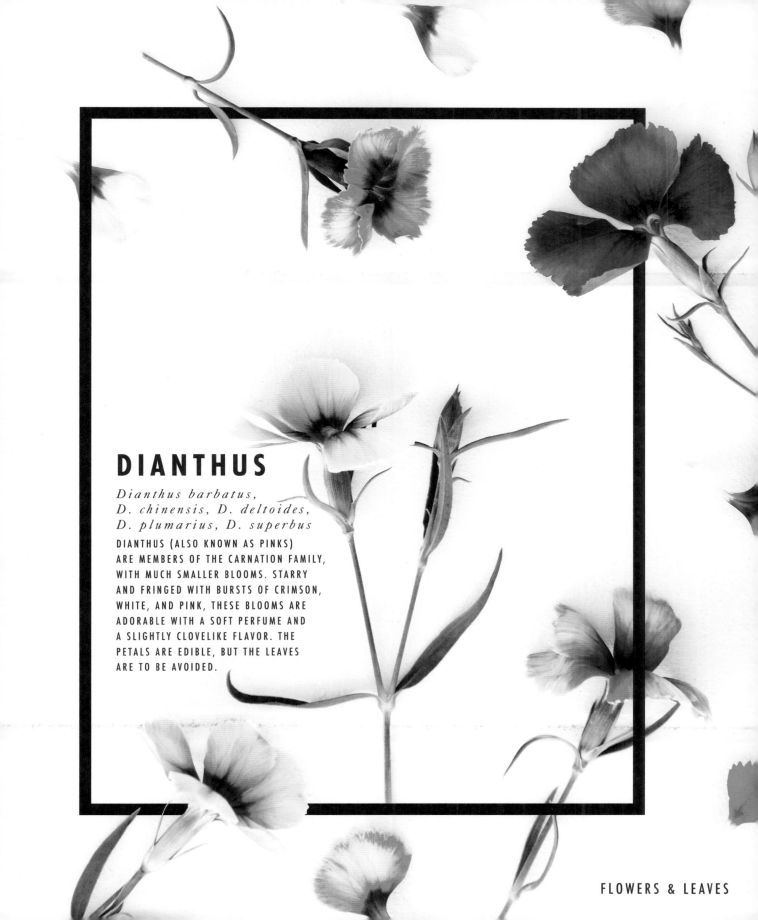

DIANTHUS

Dianthus barbatus,
D. chinensis, D. deltoides,
D. plumarius, D. superbus

DIANTHUS (ALSO KNOWN AS PINKS)
ARE MEMBERS OF THE CARNATION FAMILY,
WITH MUCH SMALLER BLOOMS. STARRY
AND FRINGED WITH BURSTS OF CRIMSON,
WHITE, AND PINK, THESE BLOOMS ARE
ADORABLE WITH A SOFT PERFUME AND
A SLIGHTLY CLOVELIKE FLAVOR. THE
PETALS ARE EDIBLE, BUT THE LEAVES
ARE TO BE AVOIDED.

172

ELDERFLOWER
Sambucus nigra

TINY SCENTED, CREAM FLOWERS AND
FEATHERY LEAVES MAKE
THE ELDERFLOWER A JEWEL IN
ANY GARDEN. I LOVE THEIR
DELICATE AND ELEGANT NATURE.
USE ONLY THE FLOWERS.
WARNING: ELDERFLOWER CAN HAVE A
DIURETIC EFFECT, SO IT SHOULD
BE AVOIDED BY PREGNANT
AND LACTATING WOMEN.

FUCHSIA

Fuchsia × hybrida

THE FLAMBOYANT FUCHSIA, WITH ITS STRIKING
AND EXOTIC TWO-TONED BLOOMS IN A RANGE
OF PINKS, REDS, AND PURPLES, IS AS UNUSUAL
AS IT IS DELICATE. THE FLOWER IS SLIGHTLY
ACIDIC, BUT SWEET TO TASTE. YOU WILL LOVE
USING THESE GRACEFUL BLOOMS TO
DECORATE YOUR CAKES.

174

SCENTED GERANIUM

Pelargonium spp.

THERE ARE OTHER VARIETIES OF GERANIUM, BUT IT IS ONLY
THE SCENTED GERANIUM LEAVES AND FLOWERS THAT ARE
EDIBLE. THE FLOWER ITSELF HAS NO PERFUME AND IT'S THE
THICK AND HAIRY LEAVES AND LEAF HAIRS THAT PRODUCE
AND RELEASE THE DELICIOUSLY FRAGRANT SCENT. THE LEAVES
CAN BE ROUND OR FINELY CUT AND LACY IN APPEARANCE.
SCENTED GERANIUMS COME IN AN ENORMOUS VARIETY OF
COLORS AND FLAVORS AND VARY IMMENSELY,
FROM ROSE TO LEMON TO MINT.

HIBISCUS

Hibiscus rosa-sinensis

THESE DAZZLING TROPICALS HAVE
FIVE PETALS, WHICH CURL BACK FROM
THEIR CENTERS AND DROOP GRACEFULLY.
SOME ARE FRILLED OR FLUTED, AND THEY
RANGE IN COLORS FROM VIBRANT PINK TO
BRIGHT YELLOW AND ORANGE. THE FLAVOR
RANGES FROM TART TO SWEET, MILDLY
CITRUS TO CRANBERRY-LIKE.
WARNING: IT'S BEST TO USE ONLY
THE PETALS FROM THE FLOWER HEADS.
IF YOU USE THEM WHOLE, REMOVE ALL
TRACES OF THE POLLEN, AS IT IS TOXIC.

176

IMPATIENS

Impatiens walleriana

THESE DELIGHTFUL BLOOMS COME IN A VARIETY OF COLORS,
INCLUDING PINK, ROSE, RED, LILAC, PURPLE, ORANGE,
WHITE, AND BI-COLORED. THE FLOWERS TASTE QUITE BLAND,
BUT THE BLOOMS ARE PRETTY AND ARE
WORTH CRYSTALLIZING. USE ONLY THE FLOWERS.

JASMINE

Jasminum officinale

THIS IS ONE OF MY FAVORITE FLOWERS — EVERY YEAR I LONG FOR JASMINE SEASON. THE
BLOOMS ARE VERY SWEET TO TASTE AND INTENSELY FRAGRANT. THE PLANT IS A TWINING
CLIMBER WITH SHARPLY POINTED LEAVES AND TINY, STARRY WHITE BLOOMS. THEIR DIVINELY
HEADY SCENT WOULD BE WELCOME AT ANY TABLE. ONLY THE FLOWERS ARE EDIBLE.

KALE

Brassica oleracea 'Acephala'

A HARDY MEMBER OF THE BRASSICACEAE CABBAGE FAMILY, THIS VEGETABLE IS A NON-HEADING PLANT WITH CURLY OR STRAIGHT BLUE-GREEN TO PURPLE LEAVES. ITS ATTRACTIVE FOLIAGE MAKES FOR A SPECTACULAR GARNISH FOR A CAKE. IT'S EDIBLE, BUT IT'S UNLIKELY YOU WILL WANT TO EAT IT WITH A SWEET CAKE.

LAVENDER

Lavandula multifida, L. stoechas, L. angustifolia, L. dentata

AROMATIC LAVENDER FLOWERS ARE BORNE ON WIRY, SLENDER SPIKES AT THE ENDS OF
WOODY STEMS. THE BLOOMS MAY BE BLUE, BUT ARE MOST COMMONLY VIOLET OR LILAC.
OCCASIONALLY THEY CAN BE BLACKISH PURPLE, WHITE, OR EVEN YELLOWISH. THEIR RESINY
FLOWER HEADS SHOULD BE USED ONLY IN SMALL AMOUNTS AS THE FLAVOR AND PERFUME
CAN BE OVERWHELMING. THEY ARE GREAT CRYSTALLIZED.

MINT

Mentha × piperita, M. pulegium, M. suaveolens,
M. × gracilis, M spicata

FLOWERS OF THE MINT FAMILY TASTE LIKE THEIR LEAVES, BUT SOMEWHAT MILDER,
AND ARE GENERALLY WHITE, PINK, OR MAUVE. THE BLOOMS ARE REFRESHING AND UPLIFTING
WHEN ACCOMPANIED BY THEIR LEAVES AND MAKE AN APPEALING DISPLAY ON A CAKE.

182

NASTURTIUM

Tropaeolum majus, T. minus

THIS SOFT AND SPRAWLING PLANT IS KNOWN FOR ITS VIBRANT ORANGE AND YELLOW FLOWERS AND BRIGHT GREENERY. IT'S SO EASY TO GROW — IN FACT, IN SOME AREAS IT'S CONSIDERED A PEST. NASTURTIUM FLOWERS, LEAVES, SEEDS, AND SEED PODS ARE ALL EDIBLE. THEY HAVE A TANGY, PEPPERY FLAVOR.

PANSY

Viola × wittrockiana

LARGER THAN THEIR VIOLET SISTERS,
PANSIES ARE DELIGHTFUL BLOOMS.
MILD, SWEET, AND LETTUCE-LIKE TO
TART IN FLAVOR, THESE FLOWERS
CAN BE FOUND IN A MULTITUDE OF
COLORS, THE MOST COMMON BEING
WHITE, PINK, AND VIOLET. THESE
ARE VERY POPULAR CRYSTALLIZED.
EAT ONLY THE PETALS.

ROSE

Rosa spp.

THE ROSE IS PROBABLY THE MOST ADORED FLOWER OF ALL. ALL VARIETIES
AND SPECIES CAN BE USED. ROSES COME IN A RAINBOW OF COLORS AND
SIZES WITH A DISTINCTIVE AND CAPTIVATING PERFUME. THE STRONGER
THE SCENT, THE STRONGER THE FLAVOR WILL BE. ROSES ARE LOVELY
CRYSTALLIZED. BE SURE TO REMOVE THE BITTER WHITE PORTION
OF THE PETALS AND, OF COURSE, BEWARE OF THE THORNS.

186

ROSEMARY

Rosmarinus officinalis

ROSEMARY IS AN EVERGREEN, WOODY SHRUB WITH AROMATIC,
NEEDLELIKE LEAVES. THE BLUE, MAUVE, OR PINK FLOWERS HAVE A PUNGENT
FRAGRANCE, REMINISCENT OF PINE. THE FLOWERS ARE SLIGHTLY SWEET.

SAGE

Salvia officinalis

AN AROMATIC CULINARY AND MEDICINAL
HERB WITH SOFT AND FUZZY GRAYISH
LEAVES AND WOODY STEMS. THE LOVELY
FLOWER SPIKES ARE BLUE TO PURPLE.

SNAPDRAGON

Antirrhinum majus

THE FLOWERS OF THE SNAPDRAGON ARE PRODUCED ON A TALL SPIKE. THE COMMON NAME ORIGINATES FROM THE FLOWERS' REACTION TO HAVING THEIR "THROATS" SQUEEZED, WHICH CAUSES THE "MOUTH" OF THE FLOWER TO SNAP LIKE A DRAGON'S JAW. WILD SNAPDRAGONS ARE OFTEN PINK TO PURPLE WITH YELLOW LIPS. THESE DELICATE, EDIBLE BLOOMS VARY FROM BLAND TO BITTER IN TASTE. **WARNING:** WHEN FORAGING, YOU MAY FIND TRAPPED INSECTS WITHIN THE FLOWER — BE SURE TO LOOK FOR THEM AND REMOVE THEM.

STRAWBERRY

Fragaria × ananassa, F. vesca

THE COMMON GARDEN STRAWBERRY IS
A ROSETTE-FORMING PERENNIAL SPREAD BY THIN
RUNNERS, WITH DARK GREEN LEAVES THAT ARE
HAIRY ON THE UNDERSIDES. THE DAINTY FLOWERS
HAVE FIVE PETALS AND ARE GENERALLY WHITE
OR PINK WITH A YELLOW CENTER. THE FLOWERS
MAINTAIN THE SCENT AND FLAVOR OF THE FRUIT,
BUT ARE SOMEWHAT MILDER. THIS IS ANOTHER
FLOWER THAT IS GREAT TO CRYSTALLIZE. USE
BOTH THE FRUIT AND FLOWERS. THE LEAVES
ARE EDIBLE BUT ASTRINGENT.

190

THYME

Thymus spp.

A CULINARY AND ORNAMENTAL HERB WITH SMALL, DELICATE NARROW LEAVES AND WOODY,
REDDISH GRAY-BROWN STEMS. THIS HERB HAS A PENETRATING AND HEADY FRAGRANCE.
THE FLOWERS CAN BE PINK, WHITE, OR LAVENDER, DEPENDING ON THE SPECIES.

FLOWER CONFETTI

FLOWER CONFETTI IS EXACTLY WHAT IT SOUNDS LIKE — CONFETTI MADE FROM
FLOWERS. BERGAMOT (BEE BALM), BORAGE, CALENDULA, CHRYSANTHEMUM,
CORNFLOWER, AND DAISY PETALS ARE A PARTICULARLY LOVELY COMBINATION,
OR YOU CAN CREATE YOUR OWN MIX. THIS MAKES A GORGEOUS DECORATION
FOR YOUR CAKE AND, OF COURSE, IS ALSO GREAT FOR WEDDINGS. I LOVE A CAKE
TOPPED WITH CHANTILLY CREAM (PAGE 130) AND FLOWER CONFETTI SCATTERED
OVER THE TOP. IT'S SIMPLE, COLORFUL, AND EFFECTIVE.

PART
04

SETTING
THE SCENE

Handmade
decorations

EVERYONE KNOWS that the key to an unforgettable event is the decorations, right? However, these days the decorations can be the first thing on the party-planning list to be ditched for lack of funds. Well, here are some super-easy, ultra-fabulous DIY projects that you can create in an afternoon for very little outlay – you might even have all the materials you need lying around at home. Impress your guests while enjoying the pleasure that comes from making something with your own hands.

196

SIMPLE GREEN CHANDELIER

Move the flowers off the table and into the air, and wow your guests with your cleverness! A simple yet elegant green chandelier, or hanging wreath, made of foliage or flora (or both) makes a lush statement at any event. You can use simple flat pine to start and later get braver and try some long, attractively unruly foliage. Choose colors and textures that harmonize with the color palette for your function.

YOU WILL NEED

greenery of choice (flat pine featured here)

embroidery hoop (here I have
used an 18-inch hoop)

floral wire (green)

garden shears

jute string or natural twine

gold curtain ring

01 Examine your greenery and select the most attractive, blemish-free pieces to use. You will need 8- to 12-inch lengths. Remove any dead or scraggy bits.

02 Take your embroidery hoop, a stem of greenery, and about 4 inches of floral wire. Attach the greenery at the lower part of the stem by wrapping the floral wire around the hoop and greenery, then twisting firmly and tightly as close to the hoop as possible. You may need to attach several pieces of wire along the length of the stem of greenery. Always consider the placement of the wire – you want to camouflage it where possible with the greenery.

03 With your next piece of greenery, feed the stem under the foliage of the last piece. You may like to trim the stem with your shears if it is too long. Stems are best concealed in most instances. Secure with floral wire and repeat these steps until your hoop is completely covered.

04 Trim all your floral wire. Turn your hoop upright to view and check it. Trim any irregular foliage for a uniform look and check for gaps. Trim some offcuts from your leftover pieces and use them to fill any gaps in your wreath. Attach the pieces with floral wire and trim again with shears.

05 To hang the chandelier, measure your string to four times the width of your hoop. Cut the string in half, into two pieces the same length. Imagining your hoop as a clock face, take one of the pieces of string and tie one end to your hoop at 9 o'clock. Then thread the string through the gold ring and tie the other end to the opposite side at 3 o'clock. Don't tie and knot the string too tightly, as you might need to adjust it slightly when hanging.

06 Now tie the other length of string at 12 o'clock and at 6 o'clock, making sure to thread the string through the gold ring.

07 Take the gold ring and suspend the chandelier from a ceiling hook, or attach it to another piece of string to wrap around a tree branch in an outdoor setting. Stand back and check that the chandelier is level – adjust the strings if necessary by loosening or tightening. Try to center the chandelier if you are hanging it over a table. If using multiple chandeliers, make sure they are centered and evenly spaced.

03

05

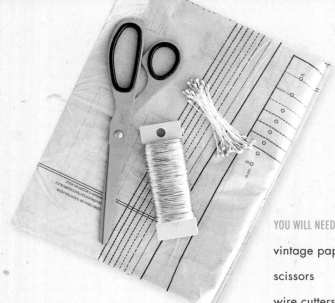

VINTAGE PAPER FLOWERS

Here is a way to use vintage dressmaking patterns, which you can find at secondhand stores or online. Delve inside the packets to discover the beautiful sepia tissue paper, perfect for some old-world charm. Here I have added store-bought millinery stamens for added effect – these can be found in the millinery section of your craft store in a range of colors, and are quite inexpensive. I make these flowers while sitting in front of the television. They are easy and can look very effective in the right setting.

IDEAS FOR USE...

I LOVE THESE PAPER FLOWERS IN A VASE, USING CORKSCREW WILLOW FOR THE STEMS. THEY ALSO LOOK LOVELY AS AN ADORNMENT FOR A WRAPPED GIFT, TIED TO THE BACK OF A PARTY CHAIR, USED AS PART OF A PAPER GARLAND, OR EVEN TO MAKE A DOOR GARLAND USING VARIED SIZES.

YOU WILL NEED

vintage paper dressmaking patterns

scissors

wire cutters

millinery stamens

jewelry wire (fine)

twigs (if making the flowers to display in a vase as a floral arrangement)

01 Open out a pattern piece. Measure and cut it into four 8 x 20-inch strips. Layer the strips on top of one another.

02 Accordion-fold the paper to the end of the strip. Set aside.

03 Cut a 6-inch length of jewelry wire. Wrap it around the center of the stamens. Twist the wire firmly to secure. (How many stamens you use is up to you – I generally like to use 8–10 per flower.)

04 Attach the stamens to the center of the folded paper. Wrap the wire around and twist it at the base.

05 Fan open the paper and stamens.

06 Working first with one side of the fan, separate the top layer of the paper from the rest, pulling it gently and slowly away, starting at the ends and pulling toward the center. Work slowly and carefully so as not to rip the delicate paper.

07 After the first layer is separated, begin on the second layer, doing the same thing on each layer until one half of the flower is full and rounded. Repeat the step for the other side of the flower.

02

04

06

200

POLISH CHANDELIER

This is an adaptation of the age-old Polish chandelier, or pajaki, traditionally crafted from paper or straw, central to the Christmas and Easter celebrations of Polish peasants, and hung over the feasting table. My simple version here uses paper and straws with the addition of faux flowers and ribbons. I selected roses and hibiscus, but use flowers to match your chosen color palette.

YOU WILL NEED

20 assorted small faux flowers

20 assorted large faux flowers

wire cutters

7-inch wire circle

11½-inch wire circle

white crêpe paper or floral tape

12 faux leaves (leaves grouped in threes are best)

4 x 9½-inch clear drinking straws, each cut into 5 equal lengths

4 x 14-inch lengths of jewelry wire

4 equal lengths of thin ribbon for hanging

01 Remove the flowers and leaves from your faux flower stems and discard the stems. You will find removal easy, as the blooms and leaves should just slide off or unplug. The larger blooms are to sit on the frame or wire circles of the chandelier, and the smaller blooms and leaves are for the supporting threads of the chandelier.

02 Cover your two wire circles with crêpe paper or tape, by wrapping it around the wire and securing.

03 Take your leaves, small blooms, and straws for the supporting threads, and divide into four equal piles.

04 Start with a leaf and one of the 14-inch lengths of wire. Thread a leaf on the wire, then a piece of cut straw and then a small flower. Repeat with the pieces of straw and flowers and finish with another leaf at the other end. Make sure that your leaves and small blooms all face in the same

direction when you thread them, and that each thread looks the same – continuity is important for an aesthetically pleasing result. Repeat for the other three strands. Ensure you have a little wire at both ends that you can use to wrap around the paper-covered wire circles in the next step.

05 Take the smaller paper-covered wire circle and attach the four strands of flowers to it by wrapping one wire end around the small circle. Attach the other end of the four flower strands to the large wire circle. If you imagine your circles as clock faces, you will be wrapping the wire threads around them at 10, 2, 4, and 8 o'clock. Be careful when attaching the threads that your blooms don't slide off your wire. The smaller wire circle goes at the top of the chandelier. Wrap the four lengths of ribbon for hanging the chandelier around the top smaller wire circle at 12, 3, 6, and 9 o'clock. It's best to hang the chandelier now, before you add the large flowers. It will also make it easier to adjust the lengths of your wire threads so your chandelier hangs evenly. Expect to make adjustments.

06 Starting at the points where the threads meet the circles at each end, attach the larger flowers with floral wire or hot glue. If you are using floral wire, be careful that it doesn't show. Embellish your chandelier further, if desired.

201

04

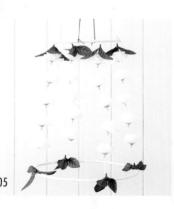

05

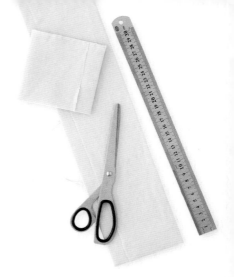

CRÊPE PAPER FLOWERS

Crêpe paper flowers capture the essence and beauty of real blooms without the botanical details – well, mine do anyway! These are the simplest of versions, perfect for the beginner, so don't be intimidated. They are inexpensive and make for a bright and cheery visual statement. After learning this simple skill, you can let your imagination run free. Choosing a variety of styles and colors creates interest – add a few strips of trailing crêpe paper. You can buy a roll of streamers or just make your own. Adding ribbons, a pom-pom garland (page 221), or the odd artificial flower looks especially pretty.

IDEAS FOR USE...

ONCE YOU PERFECT THESE, EXPERIMENT WITH LAYERING COLORS. WHY NOT MAKE MASSES OF THESE (WHILE WATCHING A MOVIE MARATHON) TO CREATE A STUNNING BACKDROP FOR A PARTY TABLE, OR JUST TO BE SCATTERED ON TIMBER OR WHITE FLOORS FOR IMPACT. MAKE A GARLAND FOR THE CENTER OF A WIDE TABLE, OR PLACE THEM AROUND A FRAME FOR A FUN PARTY PHOTO BOOTH IDEA. CHECK OUT THE FLAMBOYANT DOOR DECORATION AND THE POLISH CHANDELIER I CREATED FOR THE FIESTA STORY ON PAGES 234, 237, AND 239.

YOU WILL NEED

1 package of crêpe paper
(the package I used measured
14 x 4 inches)

scissors

ruler

fine jewelry wire

01 Cut the crêpe paper into five equal lengths across. This will give you five 2¾-inch lengths of 4-inch widths.

02 Unravel each length into one long strip of crêpe paper and then cut the single strip into four equal lengths.

03 Accordion-fold the paper at ¾-inch intervals until you have folded the full length of the paper.

04 Tie a little wire around the center of the folded crêpe paper. Be firm but do not pull – you don't want to rip the paper. Fan out the paper like a butterfly.

05 Working first with one side of the fan, separate the top layer of the paper from the rest, pulling gently and slowly away, starting at the ends and pulling toward the center. Work slowly and be careful not to rip the paper. After the first layer is separated, begin on the second layer, doing the same thing on each layer until one half of the flower is full and rounded. Repeat the step for the other side of the flower. Once finished, gently move the layers to even them out if necessary.

03

04

05

01

02

04

05

tissue paper

scissors

ruler

floral wire

ribbon of choice to hang the garland

01 Fold a piece of tissue paper in half. Here I have used a folded strip 24 inches in length, to make a 12-inch drop. Cut the strips toward the fold to create a fringe, leaving about 1 inch uncut at the fold line.

02 Unfold the tissue paper. Begin rolling down the middle crease. After a couple of rolls, add a cut piece of floral wire to the length of the middle section of uncut paper. Keep rolling the paper until you reach the end. It's not essential to use wire, but I find it makes for a neater and more uniform finish.

03 Twist the paper around the wire.

04 Now bend the wire and cross over the loop then twist to secure. You may like to use a glue gun here to secure, but generally the wire will hold firmly in place.

05 Repeat until you have the desired number of tassels for your garland. The length of ribbon you require will depend on the number of tassels you make. Suspend your garland by attaching it from both ends with a hook or nail. Allow for a little slack or drooping for best visual appeal.

TISSUE PAPER TASSEL GARLAND

Handmade tassel garlands are festive decorations for any occasion. Make them with tissue paper to match your party's color palette with a few sparkling paper ones thrown in, and you will really set the scene. These garlands are light and easy to hang and so simple to make, you can even rope in the kids to help. There are multiple uses for these garlands – use them as a train attached to a helium balloon, or hang them over the back of a chair.

IDEAS FOR USE...

THESE GARLANDS ARE GREAT SCENE-SETTERS WHEN STRUNG ON A WALL BEHIND A DESSERT PARTY TABLE, DRINKS TABLE, OR PARTY BUFFET. MAKE SEVERAL GARLANDS IN COLORS TO MATCH YOUR CHOSEN PALETTE AND SUSPEND THEM OVER ALL THE TABLES AT YOUR EVENT.

206

ORIGAMI WISHING BOATS

These origami paper boats make gorgeous "wishing boats" for a special occasion, such as a wedding or other celebratory event held near a river or lake. You make the boats, place a tea light candle in each one, light the candles, and then launch the boats into the water while making a wish. They are most effective at night, and a large number of these being launched at the same time looks amazing!

YOU WILL NEED

colorful paper suitable for origami (I have used a 6 x 8-inch sheet)

tea light candles (optional)

01 Begin with a rectangular piece of paper, colored-side up. Fold the paper in half upwards.

02 Now fold the left and right bottom corners upwards to meet in the center.

03 Fold the top layer of paper downwards over the two folded corners. Flip and do the same on the other side.

04 Hold the paper, point facing down. Grab the top by both sides and open it out as far as it will go, so you have an even smaller square shape. Flatten.

05 Fold the top corner of the top layer down to the bottom. Flip and do the same on the other side.

06 Hold the paper, point facing down, and grab the top again by both sides and open out as far as it will go, so you have a small square. Flatten.

07 Hold the square with the folded corner at the top and gently pull the top apart to make a boat shape. The upright triangle inside will be the internal "sail."

08 Lie the boat on its side and flatten well. If you want to fill the boat with a tea light candle or other items, open the boat and tuck the internal sail to one side and under the lip of the fold of paper. Now you are ready to sail and launch your wish.

IDEAS FOR USE...
IN THE SIMPLE ECO WEDDING STORY ON PAGE 250, I MADE THE BOATS IN DECORATIVE PAPER TO MATCH THE COLOR PALETTE OF THE EVENT. THEN I PUT IN A TEA LIGHT CANDLE AS WELL AS SOME FOLIAGE TO MATCH THE OTHER FLORAL DECORATIONS.

01

03

05

PAPER DOT GARLAND

Paper dot garlands are delightfully pretty and can be easily created to suit your theme and color palette. You can make these with stunning printed or plain card stock, gift wrap, or even metallic paper for a little bling!

209

01 Cut circles out of your chosen paper
using the cutter.

02 Cut the linen thread to the desired length
for your garland.

03 Place the thread across the middle of a circle,
horizontally. Then glue another circle directly on
top of the first circle, on top of the thread. You
will have two circles joined together with your
thread for the garland running through the middle.
Continue, spacing the circles evenly or randomly,
as you wish, until you reach the desired length
for your garland.

YOU WILL NEED

colored paper/card

circle paper cutter

scissors

linen thread

craft glue

IDEAS FOR USE...
THESE PAPER DOT GARLANDS WORK WELL AS A STAND-ALONE
DECORATION, OR MIXED WITH OTHER DECORATIONS.
SEE PAGE 248, WHERE I HAVE USED ONE TO DECORATE THE
BACKDROP IN THE SIMPLE ECO WEDDING STORY.

210

PAPER FAN GARLAND

This is a more feminine style of garland made from paper fans with rounded edges. Here I have used an inexpensive wrapping paper, but you could select something more elegant if you desire. Go and wow your guests with one of these garlands and touch their hearts with the effort you have made.

YOU WILL NEED

paper of choice

scissors

ruler

craft glue

ribbon

01 Cut a 12-inch square from your paper. Accordion-fold the paper at ¾-inch intervals. Repeat until you reach the end of the paper.

02 Fold the piece of paper in half and then glue the inside of the folded paper as shown. Press firmly to secure.

03 Cut the edges of the folded paper into a rounded shape. Don't be too concerned if it's not perfect. Cutting all the layers exactly in this process is difficult

04 With the fan folded, take your scissors and cut a small triangular wedge halfway along the fold – you can do this wherever you like, and you could also cut more than one wedge.

05 Open the folded paper and reveal your fan.

06 Make more! Make them all the same or try a variety of different sizes. Cut the triangular wedge into some but not all. Let your creativity shine through

07 Attach your fans to your chosen ribbon by gluing the top lip of the paper to the ribbon to create a garland. If you find you have made a few too many folds, and the fans do not sit well, then just glue the top folds where needed for a neater finish.

IDEAS FOR USE...

PAPER FAN GARLANDS ARE A LOVELY DECORATION FOR A GARDEN SOIRÉE, BIRTHDAY PARTY, GRADUATION, OR BRIDAL SHOWER. SEE THE BABY SHOWER STORY ON PAGE 231, WHERE I MADE PAPER FANS WITH A COMBINATION OF INEXPENSIVE PAPER AND A MORE GLITZY DESIGN.

01

02

04

212

PLEATED PAPER PINWHEEL

I just love pinwheels. They are easy to make and are a wonderful way of creating some serious eye candy at any event.

IDEAS FOR USE...
MY FAVORITE USE FOR THESE IS AS A BACKDROP FOR
A WEDDING TABLE (SEE THE ECO WEDDING STORY, PAGE 248),
OR FOR A DESSERT TABLE AT A PARTY. YOU COULD ALSO PLACE
THEM AROUND A LARGE FRAME FOR A FUN PHOTO BOOTH AT
AN EVENT — THIS WILL ENCOURAGE YOUR GUESTS TO STRIKE
A POSE. USE THEM TO ADORN GIFT WRAPPING (SEE PAGE 228),
SUSPEND THEM OVER TABLES, OR USE THEM AS KIDS' PARTY
FAVORS WITH SOME TRAILING RIBBON OR STREAMERS.
THEY CAN ALSO BE PLACED ON BAMBOO SKEWERS AND
USED AS A CAKE TOPPER.

213

YOU WILL NEED

scissors

3 sheets of scrapbook paper

ruler

craft glue

stapler

thread (optional)

01 Cut your paper into squares. Accordion-fold the paper at ¾-inch intervals. Apply pressure to the folded piece of paper for neat and defined fold marks. Scrapbook paper can vary in thickness and a little extra pressure for heavy card stock will make for a better finish.

02 Fold each piece of paper in half and secure with glue. This creates part of the pinwheel. Repeat twice more — three fans are needed for one pinwheel.

03 Attach all three fans to each other, using glue to secure, and then staple at the edge of the pinwheel for added strength and reliability.

04 If you want to hang the pinwheel, staple some thread to the top.

03

04

214

TISSUE PAPER POM-POM

Tissue paper pom-poms make simple, inexpensive, and effective decorations. You can use them for birthday parties, children's parties, weddings, or just because. Here, I have used one packet of tissue paper to make two 8-inch pom-poms. If you like, you can make pom-poms in varied sizes – make them with five to ten layers of 8 x 16-inch or 8 x 20-inch sheets of tissue paper. Ten layers always works best for the larger sizes. Once you try one, you will discover how many layers you prefer and how many pom-poms you can make from your packet of tissue paper.

01 Unfold your tissue paper. Carefully iron the paper on a very low heat setting to remove all the creases, if necessary. Cut the tissue paper into 8-inch squares. I have made ten layers – five layers for each pom-pom, making two pom-poms this size per package of tissue paper. Accordion-fold the paper at 1½-inch intervals. Keep folding until you get to the end of the piece of paper.

02 Place a length of ribbon around the center of the paper and tie firmly but don't pull – you don't want to rip the tissue paper.

03 Unfold and fan out the folded tissue paper on one side, making sure the ribbon is centered so the fan is of equal length on both sides.

04 Working first with one side of the fan, separate the top layer of tissue paper from the rest, pulling it gently and slowly away, starting at the ends and pulling toward the center. Work slowly and carefully so as not to rip the tissue.

05 After the first layer is separated, begin on the second layer, doing the same thing on each layer until one half of the pom-pom is full and rounded. Hold the inside center of the pom-pom where the ribbon is tied and turn the pom-pom upside down.

06 Repeat steps 4 and 5 on the reverse side until you have one full pom-pom. If needed, gently move the layers to even the pom-pom out. Make another pom-pom with the additional five layers. Voila!

07 Hang the pom-poms with the ribbon to decorate any way you please.

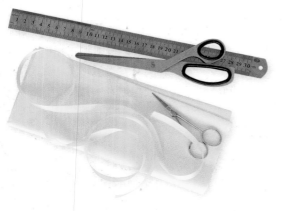

YOU WILL NEED

tissue paper

scissors

ruler

ribbon

.IDEAS FOR USE...

TIE THEM TO THE BACKS OF CHAIRS, BUNCH THEM AROUND A DOOR FRAME TO MAKE A STATEMENT ENTRANCE, USE THEM TO ADORN GIFT WRAPPING, GLUE THEM TO THE TOP OF BAMBOO SKEWERS, OR ADD THEM TO VASES AS FUN FAUX FLOWERS – A FEW TRAILING RIBBONS MAKE A NICE TOUCH. THEY WILL MAKE A GREAT CAKE CROWN OR TOPPING, OR EVEN A CROWN FOR YOU – ATTACHED TO A HEADBAND OR BRACELET, THESE ARE FUN FOR KIDS' PARTIES, AND GIRLS LOVE THEM!

01

02

04

BOBBIN CANDLESTICKS

I frequent my local antiques stores and often see baskets of vintage wooden textile bobbins, which I think are truly beautiful. Here is a way to repurpose these now seemingly useless objects into alluring candlesticks for the home or for an event with an old-fashioned feel. The bobbins come in a variety of sizes and some have painted edges. Here I have chosen some with a simple, metal-banded edge. Always check that they have a flat base for stability. Select taper candles for an elegant look, or small pillar candles for a more robust design.

217

YOU WILL NEED

vintage wooden textile bobbins

craft or wood glue

taper or pillar candles to fit your chosen bobbins

01 Choose which end of your bobbin you wish to glue your candle to. I recommend you select the larger surface area if you have a choice.

02 Place a drop of glue at the end of your candle and press the candle firmly down onto the bobbin. Hold in place until you feel the glue has bonded.

03 Leave to dry. Simple!

IDEAS FOR USE...

BOBBIN CANDLESTICKS ARE A GREAT CONVERSATION PIECE AT AN EVENT, AND THEY ALSO MAKE LOVELY GIFTS. CHECK OUT PAGE 242, WHERE I USED THESE BOBBIN CANDLESTICKS IN THE SIMPLE ECO WEDDING STORY AS BOTH RUSTIC TABLE DECORATIONS AND SOFT LIGHTING.

218

YARN POM-POMS

Over the years I have made many a pom-pom. I have used cardboard templates and tried my hand at a few kinds of pom-pom kits. While I love a great kit, all you really need is some wool and a fork. Yes, a fork. Having said this, the fork method only lends itself to small pom-poms of about 2 inches. For larger ones (or if you are a perfectionist), you are better off using a kit. The fork method makes pom-poms with slight irregularities but, personally, I find the imperfections charming.

YOU WILL NEED

yarn (a 3-ply works well)

dinner fork (with 4 prongs)

small sharp scissors (embroidery scissors are ideal)

wire (optional)

01 Take a fork and position it upright. Thread the yarn through the two middle prongs. Start to wrap the yarn around the width and base of the prongs. Wrap it five times. This is your guide for the width of your wrapping for your pom-pom.

02 Continue to wrap the yarn about 35 times, being mindful not to exceed ½ inch in width.

03 Use the scissors to cut your yarn, then tie the two loose strands together.

04 Cut a 4-inch length of yarn and carefully slide the yarn through the two middle prongs of the fork at the base. Wrap the yarn around the middle of the wrapped yarn on the fork and tie it very firmly – a loose tie will bring everything unstuck! Once tied, it should resemble a bow shape. If you are finding tying the yarn around the middle of the fork difficult, then this is where you can use the wire as an option to secure the yarn tightly. Trim the hanging yarn.

05 Turning the fork on its side, holding it in one hand and resting it in the other, firmly hold the yarn. With sharp scissors (don't attempt this with blunt ones!), cut the yarn along the side of the fork. Remember to hold the wool in place. Take your time cutting through the layers.

06 Turn your fork over and repeat the process of cutting along the fork's edge.

07 Slide your pom-pom gently off the fork. Fluff the yarn out with your fingers. Now trim your pom-pom as evenly as possible into a ball. Start trimming the outside threads to form the shape. You may have irregular threads, but don't worry as the pom-pom doesn't need to be perfect. Remember, after trimming, your pom-pom will end up significantly smaller.

IDEAS FOR USE...
THESE ARE FUN AND WHIMSICAL AND TAKE ME STRAIGHT BACK TO MY CHILDHOOD. A FEW SCATTERED POM-POMS CAN LOOK A TREAT ON A TABLE. CHOOSE COLORS TO SUIT YOUR PARTY PALETTE.

01

02

05

07

YARN POM-POM FLOWERS

These are super-cute, easy to make, and they won't wilt. I have used store-bought yarn pom-poms, which I found at a discount store. Of course, you can make your own by following the instructions on page 218. I love to attach the yarn pom-poms to bamboo skewers as stems, then use "flowers" of varied sizes in floral arrangements.

YOU WILL NEED

yarn pom-poms, store-bought or handmade (see page 218)

bamboo skewers or fine branches

a glue gun or craft glue

01 Place a large drop of craft glue on the top of a skewer or branch. Press firmly to adhere and set. Repeat as needed.

POM-POM
GARLAND

Pom-pom garlands are a fun project for a rainy day. They are sweet and playful. If you are not into making these from scratch (see page 218), then opt for store-bought ones. Using different-sized pom-poms makes for a more whimsical look.

YOU WILL NEED

needle and thread

yarn pom-poms, store-bought or
handmade (see page 218)

01 Take your needle and thread your cotton through the center of your pom-pom. Repeat until the garland is your desired length. As a general guide, space your pom-poms ¾ inch to 2 inches apart for a consistent look.

VARIATION: POM-POM GARLAND CAKE TOPPER Make a miniature pom-pom garland, attach each end to a bamboo skewer, and then use as a cake topper – allow about 2 inches of thread at each end for tying. Make sure you allow for a little slack or droop in the garland – but not too much, though, you as don't want your pom-poms touching the cake.

221

IDEAS FOR USE...

POM-POM GARLANDS ARE LOVELY PLACED ALONG THE CENTER
OF A TABLE AS A RUNNER. THEY ALSO LOOK STRIKING AS A
DOOR CURTAIN OR BACKDROP. DRAPE THEM ABOVE OR BEHIND
A DESSERT OR BUFFET TABLE. USE THEM TO DECORATE GIFTS OR
EVEN DRAPE YOUR CHRISTMAS TREE WITH THEM FOR FUN. CHECK
OUT THE FIESTA STORY (PAGE 237) AND ECO WEDDING STORY
(PAGE 248), AND SEE HOW I ADDED THEM TO A BACKDROP AND
DOOR INSTALLATION FOR VISUAL AND TEXTURAL INTEREST.

Putting it all together

I LOVE NOTHING MORE THAN
TO COMMUNICATE A STORY VISUALLY.
The following pages contain inspiration for four
themed events, designed to get your creative juices
flowing. They bring together many of the ideas I've
shared with you in this book, from cakes, fillings,
and frostings to finishing touches and decorations.
Feel free to jump outside the guidelines, though,
and create a setting that is a reflection of
your own unique self — and don't forget,
your cake should take center stage!

A PRETTY
BABY SHOWER

HERE ARE SOME IDEAS FOR A DELIGHTFUL BABY SHOWER, BASED ON
A PASTEL COLOR PALETTE AND FEATURING PLENTY OF BRIGHT,
CHEERY BLOOMS, QUIRKY TABLEWARE, AND HANDMADE DECORATIONS.

PUTTING IT ALL TOGETHER

Roses are a great choice as a styling element. They come in such a huge array of colors and sizes, from miniature to large doubles, that there are endless decorative options.

227

228

A group of friends and family coming together at a baby shower to "shower" their expectant guest of honor with gifts and their collective knowledge of parenthood is a cherished occasion for every mother-to-be. Hosting a baby shower for a friend or family member is a great way to show your support, love, and excitement – and it doesn't have to be difficult. While there are many details to consider, the styling at least can be simple yet beautiful.

Baby showers are often held at the host's home – in the living room or family room, or in the garden – or in a beautiful park in warmer months. They can be sit-down events with place settings, or something far more casual and relaxed. Plenty of room to walk around is a good idea, as this gives guests who don't know one another the chance to mingle. A comfy chair for your mother-to-be is, of course, essential!

A simple morning or afternoon gathering is perfect – I think it's safe to say that no expectant mother wants to be up late, as the latter stages of pregnancy are exhausting. Keep the numbers down – this is an intimate event by nature and the guest of honor would love to get a chance to spend time with all those who have come to support her. If you opt for a soundtrack, choose soft, soothing music playing in the background.

You might like to do as I do and match the color of the food and drink you serve to the color palette of the event. It adds another layer of interest and appeals to the senses.

COLOR PALETTE Selecting a particular color theme and then sticking to it can help you to focus your planning and styling. The theme should run tastefully throughout the entire shower, including invitations, decorations, tableware, and thank you cards. As it's a day to celebrate womanhood, soft and feminine colors are a good choice – I love a pastel palette for this occasion. Whatever you use, always keep in mind what the expectant mother would like – the style should reflect her taste. For this event I chose colors of sage, salmon, pearl, aqua, peach, and mint, with touches of rose and pink – so pretty. Choose flowers, tableware, and a cake in the same palette, and you can't go wrong. A distinct theme will create a party atmosphere and transform a home for a perfect baby shower. Your guests could even dress to suit the color palette and could wrap their gifts in paper to tone in with the theme. I decorated the gifts with a pleated paper pinwheel (see page 212 for instructions on how to make one).

FLOWERS AND DECORATIONS Decorations will set the mood. Introduce texture, or mix plains with patterns – though a subtle approach here is key. Raid your (or your friends') cupboards and look for materials that are in the chosen color palette and suit the theme. Eclectic floral china with antique cake

forks work beautifully in this charming setting. Some vintage, jeweled sherry glasses on a decorative tray add a subtle, yet festive and vintage feel.

Flowers are a must — either elaborate arrangements or simple cuttings from your garden, depending on the theme of the party and the time of year. Here, I used scattered wildflowers in a collection of varied vases — a milk glass, clear glass vase, long-stemmed vase, and bud vases. The aroma of the flowers should be subtle, as many expectant mothers are sensitive to strong scents. Rose, gardenia, jasmine, lavender, or honeysuckle are divine. If these scents are too strong, try other beauties like eucalyptus, peonies, tulips, or snapdragons, and plants with lacy foliage like Queen Anne's lace and dusty miller.

PAPER FAN GARLAND For this event I made paper fan garlands from pretty gift wrap, which I found at my local bookstore — the paper features all the colors in my chosen palette. I also used a plain, pastel paper to complement it. See page 210 for instructions on how to make your own. The garland is a simple decoration, yet looks very effective draped over doorways, hung on a wall behind the buffet table and even on stair balustrades; just use your imagination! However, you can make

231

it easier on yourself and keep your theme to one room where you can showcase all your handmade crafts and styling flair. If you are hosting the event in a park or garden, bunting looks lovely hanging from tree branches. Selecting pretty details like this, and going to the trouble of making them by hand, will make your expectant mother feel very pampered.

THE CAKE Make the event memorable with a tiered naked cake taking center stage. Place the cake on a pedestal, giving it a sense of importance. Use a few varied cake plates or pedestal designs if you are serving a variety of treats. Create a flavor profile you know the expectant mother will love. For this event I created a simple sponge cake and filled it with luscious buttercream. Delicate roses make a fitting decoration for the top. A little trailing vine at the base of the pedestal adds to the spring feel. I wanted my guests to be transported to a garden.

232

When handing around pieces of your cake or other food, why not decorate the plates with one or two striking edible blooms for a decorative touch?

A BRIGHT FIESTA

235

WHETHER YOU ARE CELEBRATING MEXICAN DAY OF THE DEAD OR CINCO DE MAYO,
OR JUST PLANNING A MEXICAN-THEMED PARTY FOR FRIENDS, THEN HERE ARE
SOME GREAT IDEAS TO GET YOU STARTED. IT'S ALL ABOUT THE COLOR!

236

Why not turn up the heat with a Mexican-inspired fiesta? It makes a wonderful, colorful celebration for family and friends, and can be enjoyed any time of year. All you need is good company, plenty of food (including a naked cake of course), and great music for dancing. Your fiesta can be traditional and spectacular, or toned back with just a few key elements that pop. Whatever your style, bright color is non-negotiable, so have fun with it!

The vibe of a Mexican fiesta is casual, so there is no need for table settings. A great choice of drinks to serve would be herbal tea, iced tea, sangria, or fresh citrus cocktail – perhaps even some Spanish red wines.

FLOWERS AND DECORATIONS Make your fiesta a sensorial experience. Flowers can set the scene by filling the room with bursts of color as well as a glorious perfume. Dress the tables with colorful votive candles and vases with small, bright blooms. Little pots of succulents also look great and even a few larger cacti at ground level add impact. Decorate the fiesta with some traditional Mexican artefacts (or at least, modern takes on them). Choose colorful glasses, tableware, and tablecloths, and scatter some cushions around.

This party is all about color, but even if you create a colorful entry to an all-white room, you are already halfway there. Perhaps the entrance to your home or garden would be a suitable place for a door garland. The one I have created here is made from crêpe paper flowers and streamers, with a colorful pom-pom garland. It dances against the white and makes for

Work smart, not hard. Choose a menu that won't make you a slave to the kitchen – everyone has come to see you, after all! Consider hiring a taco truck to serve authentic Mexican food.

a grand entrance. See page 202 for instructions on how to make the crêpe paper flowers and page 221 for the pom-pom garland.

You could also construct a simple paper Polish chandelier and then drape beads or ribbons over it, or embellish it with faux flowers and tiny, homemade pleated paper pinwheels. Be adventurous! In warmer months you could hold the fiesta outdoors and hang the chandelier from the low-hanging branches of a tree. See page 200 for instructions on how to make a Polish chandelier and page 212 for the pinwheels.

THE CAKE A cake that features some spice, or a simple, moist citrus cake soaked with a Boozy Syrup (page 137) would be great choices. You might prefer to scale back the appearance of your cake with a simple crown, or decoration, of two or three flowers only, or you might want to decorate the tiers of your cake with small, individual blooms. However, as it's customary for fiestas to be bold and flamboyant, I recommend you go all out!

Add your own personality to your chandelier. Here, I've chosen lightweight, brightly colored beads, a variety of faux flowers, and bamboo-print drinking straws.

239

A SIMPLE
ECO WEDDING

241

A WEDDING CAN BE A WONDERFUL SHOWCASE FOR YOUR CREATIVE
TALENTS. THIS ECO-INSPIRED WEDDING FEATURES HANDCRAFTED
CANDLESTICKS MADE FROM BOBBINS AND FERN FROND CHANDELIERS,
DETAILS THAT ADD FLAIR AND WILL ENCHANT THE GUESTS.

242

I feel it's important that a wedding should be, first and foremost, a reflection of the bride and groom. Personally, I love a simple, nature-inspired wedding with a bohemian heart. An eco wedding can look every bit as lush as a traditional wedding, but it will be lighter on the pocket – as well as the environment.

If you love the look of this story and are inspired to try something like it for yourself, then here are some details to get you started. (This look also translates well to a beautiful garden-party lunch or dinner.) You may find enough information here to go ahead and plan every detail of the wedding yourself. Or, you could engage an event planner to help you, which will make life a lot easier. When you have all your ideas in place, just make sure your choices all work together and that you haven't gone overboard. The last thing that you want to be worrying about on the day are all these small details, especially if it's your own wedding. The day should be about you and your partner, and you want to be able to enjoy every minute.

As this wedding theme is inspired by nature, flora is the focal point. Repetition is key, whether it's a particular flower or color, as this makes the look cohesive. I achieved this with the selection of flowers for the table, the green chandeliers, the floral garlands, and, most importantly, the cake.

COLOR PALETTE The color palette used here is natural – white and green with touches of silvery gray and gold. It's simple and classic. A gorgeous old barn was chosen as the venue for the wedding, and beautifully worn trestle tables made the perfect canvas for the decorations, place settings, and food. A beaded lace table runner added elegance and contrasted well with the timber, but you could also use a lovely plain white or cream linen tablecloth.

THE CAKE Your overall choice of venue, dress, and flowers will help you define what the personality of your cake should be. The cake I created for this event was designed to complement the bride and groom, and communicate their taste and personal style. To decorate the cake, I used a collection of edible and decorative elements. The lush green moss blankets on the table and the rustic, raw timber boards used for the cake stand transport the guests straight to a forest floor. Fresh edible rosebuds and store-bought sugar flowers in varied sizes and shapes make a garland. At the base of the cake are decorative elements of faux vine and floral tendrils, which are also repeated throughout the styling of the whole wedding. A huge sugar flower takes pride of place on top of the cake, as any crown should.

PLACE SETTINGS AND TABLE DECORATIONS

Always try your table setting elements together before the big day. Lay them out on your dining table and check that they all look beautiful. Each individual piece should work well with every other piece in the mix. Step back and view the theme and see if it is working. Trust your instincts!

For this event, the place settings were kept simple. Gold-rimmed, antique-style plates were paired with an ornate silver charger. Silver and gold were repeated to create cohesion in the theme. The cutlery used was silver, but gold would also look beautiful. A simple white linen napkin, with jute twine tied around it and a sprig of greenery or a simple bloom tucked into it, looks lovely.

Vintage Champagne glasses and crystal decanters added a sense of luxury. A decanter with dessert wine (or perhaps whiskey – or both!), paired with beautiful crystal or colored glasses matching your color theme, would be a delightful touch. Present the glasses of wine to the tables on a beautifully ornate vintage silver tray. A few scattered blooms or foliage on the tray will further add to the atmosphere.

I always love the handpicked look with an eclectic mix of objects. It's relaxed, natural, and unstructured. If it's your own wedding, perhaps there are a few treasured family antiques you could use. If you don't have the ideal things in your home cupboard, maybe a friend does. Or, alternatively, you could scour

your local antique or secondhand stores. If you don't think you will use the items again, there are many rental places that stock beautiful vintage wares for such occasions. Either way, you'll definitely have fun hunting for these items.

You can add any number of personal touches, such as decorative place cards. Why not use recycled paper, a luggage tag with a pretty ribbon, or a potted succulent wrapped in burlap and twine? A miniature wreath of aromatic thyme or rosemary would suit the rustic vibe. When writing the place cards, call on the services of a calligrapher, or ask someone with beautiful handwriting to do the honors.

For this event, I also created a large wall backdrop made from pleated paper pinwheels (see page 212), paper dot garlands (page 210), and yarn pom-pom garlands (page 221). Handmade decorations like this can easily be created to suit your color palette and mean so much more than store-bought decorations.

Use moss as a table runner — it's inexpensive and will stay lush and green for the duration of your event. Store-bought white sugar flowers complement it beautifully.

LIGHTING Lighting can make all the difference to an event. I think it's best to always dim the lights – no one likes to dine under strong lighting. Gentle light tends to soften all the elements in a space, including your guests. You will all look your best, which is what you want at a wedding, with the cameras constantly clicking!

I grouped together candlesticks with slender taper candles in colors of white, cream, and gold. Handmade candlesticks fashioned from vintage wooden bobbins and pillar candles take pride of place. They work well with the rustic aesthetic. They are complemented by the crystal on the table. A few tea light candles scattered around the room add interest, mood, and atmosphere. See page 217 for instructions on how to make your own candlesticks from wooden bobbins.

FLOWERS AND FOLIAGE Hanging flowers and foliage can look stunning at a wedding ceremony. Suspended foliage and blooms, particularly floral garlands – delicate, or big and bold with unexpected details – are fast becoming the preferred choice for the modern bride. Choose flowers that are in season as they will be cheaper, brighter, and fresher (and therefore last longer on the day). If you are confident in your choices, then visit the local flower market yourself or find yourself a florist who shares your aesthetic. If you choose the latter option, ask your florist if you can view their work to make sure you are a good match and their services will meet your needs. Florists are artisans – some will have their own specific style that they tend toward, while others can meet your every need. Don't be afraid to shop around.

Filling out your flower arrangements with foliage is an inexpensive way to increase the visual impact of your chosen blooms. Simple green chandeliers made using conifer fronds also look divine. You won't believe how easy these are to make yourself until you start. See page 197 for instructions on how to make one.

Any vessel can be a vase for flowers. In this story I've used vintage crystal Champagne glasses (a couple left over from a broken set) and pretty metallic tea lights for a little extra bling. Egg cups and sherry glasses are wonderful for single small blooms. Smaller arrangements with intricate fillers such as berries, and individual blooms at varied heights, look great.

ORIGAMI WISHING BOATS These can help create a memorable moment at a wedding. The boats are handmade origami paper boats, in which you place tea light candles and maybe some flowers or foliage. See page 206 for details on how to make them. You should make a boat for every guest, but I suggest you make extra. Each guest makes a wish for the happy couple, lights the candle, and then sends the boat down the river or stream, carrying their well wishes with them. This looks magical, especially at night, and will touch the hearts of all involved. You could use flowers instead of paper boats and the candle, which are better for the environment. Don't forget to bring a few lighters to hand around for people to light the candles.

249

250

BOHEMIAN DESSERT PARTY

253

THIS IS MY FAVORITE STYLE OF PARTY — DECADENT, MOODY, AND
OH-SO-SEXY. THE LUSH LAYERS OF TEXTURE AND BOHEMIAN TOUCHES
ADD AN AIR OF EXOTIC SOPHISTICATION.

254

I love a dessert party. Who doesn't? I like to make it a feast for all the senses, not only the taste buds. Create a night your guests will remember and want to emulate. From rustic to contemporary, simple to extravagant, a dessert party is an invitation to indulge!

COLOR PALETTE First pick your design theme and color palette. I often like to start with the linen. For this event, it was an aubergine-colored French linen tablecloth that sparked my imagination. It seemed the perfect base for a lush, exotic, and layered story. I chose a rich palette of aubergine, purples, azure, lilac, wineberry, moss green, hot pink, and peach, with touches of black, gold, and silver and the shimmer of crystal.

FLOWERS AND DECORATIONS Flowers are emotive and engage the senses, and I couldn't do without them for this design story. Luckily the season of bold spring blooms and bulbs brought the whole thing together. The scents of exquisite flowers, exotic fruits, and aromatic herbs – with hints of chocolate and liqueur – set the scene.

Candlelight was perfect to create just the right mood. I used different-sized candlesticks, vases, pedestals, and risers in a variety of styles to play with layers of height and add interest and texture. (Never be afraid to experiment. Rummage through your cupboards and find your favorite pieces to build your idea.) Salad or dessert plates, jeweled glasses, silver and gold-plated cutlery, and dessert forks were a must, as were the sultry tunes playing in the background. Glass domes were used over cakes, cheese, and large blooms. I even used moss as a table runner: randomly placed around the table, it contrasted well with all the bright colors and abundance displayed. The addition of a stuffed parrot decoration contributed unexpected humor to the tropical, exotic theme. These surprising touches all contributed to the rich layering of the event.

Can't afford to make an elaborate tiered cheese wheel for your dessert party? That's okay – a single cheese wheel can look just as stunning. Simply scatter over some fresh edible blooms.

Vintage Champagne glasses were filled with cocktails, adorned with pear slices and thyme or sweet pansies. Small details like these help make your guests feel very special. Alternatively, artisan floral teas are delightful.

THE CAKES AND DESSERTS Of course, a selection of swoon-worthy desserts to suit the season, time of day, and guests should take center stage. Offering a selection of desserts that your guests can feel free to explore is ideal. Spoil them with choice. Every cake deserves a pedestal – it adds a sense of grandeur and occasion. It also creates more space on the table to layer your scene underneath the pedestals. Items that make for beautiful, unexpected plateaus and risers for your cakes include antique sieves (wooden or metal), rustic and raw wooden slabs, and upended vintage round cake pans and hat boxes. A large, single cheese wheel on a silver riser looks stunning, as does a multi-tiered one, decorated with edible blooms or grapes, dried fruit and nuts. Simple, fresh edible blooms make beautiful crowns for your cakes – they require little fuss and will keep you out of the kitchen and mingling with your guests.

It's time to put on a frock and heels. A few scattered tea light candles, and you are ready to party! Enjoy!

258

*Every cake deserves
a pedestal – it adds a sense
of grandeur and occasion.*